NORTHERN UTE MUSIC

Da Capo Press Music Reprint Series

NORTHERN UTE MUSIC

By Frances Densmore

DA CAPO PRESS · NEW YORK · 1972

Library of Congress Cataloging in Publication Data

Densmore, Frances, 1867-1957.
 Northern Ute music.

 (Da Capo Press music reprint series)
 Reprint of the 1922 ed.. which was issued as Bulletin
75 of Smithsonian Institution. Bureau of American
Ethnology.
 1. Indians of North America—Music. 2. Ute Indians.
I. Title. II. Series: U.S. Bureau of American
Ethnology. Bulletin 75.
ML3557.D365   1972   784.7'51   72-1887₀
ISBN 0-306-70515-X

This Da Capo Press edition of *Northern Ute Music* is an
unabridged republication of the first edition published
in Washington, D.C., in 1922 as Bulletin 75 of the
Bureau of American Ethnology, Smithsonian Institution.

Published by Da Capo Press, Inc.
A Subsidiary of Plenum Publishing Corporation
227 West 17th Street, New York, New York 10011

NORTHERN UTE MUSIC

UTE USING MORACHE

SMITHSONIAN INSTITUTION
BUREAU OF AMERICAN ETHNOLOGY
BULLETIN 75

NORTHERN UTE MUSIC

BY

FRANCES DENSMORE

WASHINGTON
GOVERNMENT PRINTING OFFICE
1922

LETTER OF TRANSMITTAL

SMITHSONIAN INSTITUTION,
BUREAU OF AMERICAN ETHNOLOGY,
Washington, D. C., November 25, 1918.

SIR: I have the honor to submit herewith the accompanying manuscript, entitled "Northern Ute Music," by Frances Densmore, and to recommend its publication as a bulletin of the Bureau of American Ethnology.

Very respectfully,

J. WALTER FEWKES,
Chief.

DR. CHARLES D. WALCOTT,
Secretary of the Smithsonian Institution.

FOREWORD

The songs comprised in this memoir were recorded among the White River, Uinta, and Uncompahgre bands of Ute in 1914 and 1916, the research being conducted chiefly at Whiterocks, Utah. In number these songs are less than those of the Chippewa and Sioux previously studied by the writer,[1] yet they contain peculiarities which contribute materially to the study of Indian music. Certain songs are found which appear to be unformulated. These are described as "rudimentary songs," and a comparison between them and the accurately repeated songs forms one of the new features of the present work.

An interesting contribution to this work is comprised in the tone photographs of portions of two of these songs, taken with the phonodeik and analyzed by Dr. Dayton C. Miller, head of the department of physics, Case School of Applied Science, Cleveland, Ohio. This cooperation is gratefully acknowledged by the writer.

Acknowledgment of assistance is tendered also to Fred Mart, a member of the Ute tribe, who acted as interpreter; to employees of the Uinta and Ouray agency at Fort Duchesne and Whiterocks, Utah; and to members of the staff of the Bureau of American Ethnology.

The comparative analysis of Indian and Slovak songs was made possible by the courtesy of Mr. Ivan Daxner, secretary of the Slovenian League of America.

---

[1] Chippewa Music, Bull. 45, Bur. Amer. Ethn., Washington, 1910; Chippewa Music, II, Bull. 53, Bur. Amer. Ethn., 1913; Teton Sioux Music, Bull. 61, Bur. Amer. Ethn., 1918.

CONTENTS

ILLUSTRATIONS

9

LIST OF SONGS

ARRANGED IN ORDER OF SERIAL NUMBERS

SONGS OF THE BEAR DANCE

---

[2]These are not included in the catalogue of Indian songs.

ARRANGED IN ORDER OF CATALOGUE NUMBERS

Cata-logue No.	Title of song	No. of singer	Serial No.	Page
690	Bear dance song (a)	4	5	63
691	....do. (b)	4	6	63
692	....do. (c)	4	7	64
693	Final song of Bear dance (b)	4	17	72
694	Sun dance song (a)	4	18	82
695	....do. (b)	4	19	82
696	Parade song (a)	4	83	167
697	Hand game song (a)	4	94	167
698	....do. (f)	4	99	179
699	....do. (l)	4	102	181
700	Sun dance song (c)	9	20	83
701	Lame dance song (a)	9	39	106
702	Closing song of the Dragging-feet dance	9	45	113
703	Iron-line dance song	9	51	120
704	War song (b)	9	68	148
705	....do. (e)	9	72	151
706	Song when washing the wounded	9	77	155
707	Parade song (b)	9	84	167
708	....do. (c)	9	85	168
709	....do. (d)	9	86	168
710	Sun dance song (f)	11	23	85
711	Song used in treatment of sick (a)	11	52	132
712	....do. (b)	11	53	132
713	....do. (c)	11	54	132
714	....do. (d)	11	55	132
715	....do. (e)	11	56	133
716	....do. (f)	11	57	133
717	....do. (g)	11	58	133
718	....do. (h)	11	59	133
719	....do. (i)	11	60	134
720	Lame dance song (b)	16	40	109
721	Dragging-feet dance (a)	16	43	112
722	Tea dance song (c)	16	48	117
723	War song (c)	16	69	148
724	Scout song	16	71	150
725	Song when washing the wounded (a)	16	76	155
726	Parade song (f)	16	88	170
727	Song when begging for tobacco	16	106	189
728	Song when welcoming visitors	16	107	189
729	Serenade	16	108	191
730	Bear dance song (j)	7	14	70

Arranged in Order of Catalogue Numbers—Continued

Catalogue No.	Title of song	No. of singer	Serial No.	Page
731	Turkey dance song (a)	7	30	97
732	.....do. (b)	7	31	98
733	Tea dance song (a)	7	46	115
734	.....do. (b)	7	47	116
735	Parade song (i)	7	91	171
736	Hand game song (b)	7	95	177
737	.....do. (e)	7	98	178
738	.....do. (h)	7	101	180
739	Bear dance song (h)	6	12	69
740	.....do. (i)	6	13	69
741	Turkey dance song (c)	6	32	99
742	.....do. (d)	6	33	99
743	Woman's dance song (b)	6	37	103
744	.....do. (c)	6	38	104
745	Hand game song (d)	6	97	178
746	Dragging-feet dance (b)	18	44	113
747	War song (f)	18	73	152
748	Parade of returning warriors	18	74	'53
749	War song (g)	18	75	154
750	Scalp dance song (b)	18	79	158
751	.....do. (c)	18	80	158
752	Song used in treatment of sick (j)	25	61	136
753	.....do. (k)	25	62	137
754	.....do. (l)	25	63	137
755	.....do. (m)	25	64	138
756	.....do. (n)	25	65	138
757	.....do. (o)	25	66	139
758	"The dust of the red wagon"	1	1	58
759	War song (a)	1	67	147
760	Scalp dance song (a)	1	78	157
761	Parade song (j)	1	92	172
762	.....do.	1	93	173
763	Bear dance song (d)	5	8	65
764	.....do. (e)	5	9	66
765	.....do. (f)	5	10	67
766	.....do. (g)	5	11	68
767	Undetermined dance song (c)	5	29	89
768	Lame dance song (c)	17	41	110
769	Closing song of the Lame dance	17	42	111
770	Double dance song	17	50	119
771	Parade song (e)	17	87	169

Arranged in Order of Catalogue Numbers—Continued

Cata-logue No.	Title of song	No. of singer	Serial No.	Page
772	"Dance faster"................................	3	3	61
773	Song of Nu'šina..............................	3	4	62
774	Final song of Bear dance (a)	3	16	71
775	Bear dance song (k).........................	8	15	70
776	Double dance song (a).......................	8	49	118
777	Sun dance song (d)..........................	8	21	84
778	.....do. (e).................................	8	22	85
779	Woman's dance song (a)......................	8	36	102
780	Parade song (g).............................	21	89	170
781	Smoking song (a)............................	21	103	187
782	.....do. (b).................................	21	104	188
783	.....do. (c).................................	21	105	188
784	Yellow hair.................................	2	2	59
785	Song around a rawhide.......................	2	109	192
786	Sun dance song (g)..........................	12	24	86
787	.....do. (h).................................	12	25	86
788	Undetermined dance song (a).................	14	27	88
789	.....do. (b).................................	14	28	89
790	Turkey dance song (e).......................	15	34	100
791	.....do. (f).................................	15	35	100
792	War song (d)................................	19	70	149
793	Parade song (h).............................	19	90	171
794	War song (h)................................	20	81	159
795	.....do. (i).................................	20	82	159
796	Hand game song (c)..........................	22	96	177
797	.....do. (g).................................	22	100	180
798	Sun dance song (i)..........................	13	26	87
799	Dream song.................................	23	110	193

SPECIAL SIGNS USED IN TRANSCRIPTIONS OF SONGS

These signs are intended simply as aids to the student in becoming acquainted with the songs. They should be understood as supplementary to the descriptive analyses rather than a part of the musical notation.

+ placed above a note shows that the tone was sung slightly higher than the indicated pitch. In many instances the tones designated by this and the following sign were "unfocused tones," or were tones whose intonation varied in the several renditions of the song. The intonation of these tones was not such as to suggest the intentional use of "fractional intervals" by the singer.

— placed above a note shows that the tone was sung slightly lower than the indicated pitch.

(· placed above a note shows that the tone was prolonged slightly beyond the indicated time. This and the following sign are used only when the deviation from strict time is less than half the time unit of the song and appears to be unimportant. In many instances the duration of the tones thus marked is variable in the several renditions of the song.

·) placed above a note shows that the tone was given slightly less than the indicated time.

⌐————⌐ placed above a series of notes indicates that these tones constitute a rhythmic unit. (See footnote to Table 19.)

NAMES OF SINGERS

Number (see transcription)	Common name [1]	Ute name [2]	Number of songs recorded
1	Little Jim	To'pătšuk	5
2	Nikoree	Nikavari	2
3	Fred Mart	Native name not given	3
4	Isaacs	Magwitšint	10
5	Clark Tonner	So'nawav	5
6	Joshua Washington	Pa'tšatš	7
7	Quinance	Kwa'nantš	9
8	Areev		2
9	Charlie Saritch	Sa'ritš	10
10	Eugene Perank (Frank)	Tavi'poniš	3
11	Teddy Pageets	Pa'gitš	10
12	Andrew Frank	(See No. 10)	2
13	Fanny Provo	Sato'yum	1
14	Sidney Blueotter	Sa'vapătšuk	2
15	Chigoop	Tšigu'p	2
16	Tim Johnson	Native name not given	10
17	Paul Pegaroos		4
18	John Star	Sa'vawitopatš	6
19	Dave Weetch	Witš	2
20	Charles Mack	Native name not given	2
21	Jim Kolorow	Tšo'kwata'piyitš	4
22	Jim Pant	Pa'ant	2
23	Arkansaw	Kanav	1
24	Weeyutchee [3]	Wiyu'tš	
25	Mrs. Washington	Sa'kwiagant	6

[1] In order that the identity of the singers may be preserved, their Ute names are here given as they are commonly pronounced on the reservation.
[2] The meaning of the Ute names is given in the glossary of Ute words, pp. 18-21.
[3] This singer recorded "rudimentary songs," which are not included in the list of composed songs. The subject of rudimentary songs is considered on p. 200.

CHARACTERIZATION OF SINGERS

The oldest singers among the White River and Uinta bands are Little Jim (No. 1), a subchief under Red Cap, leader of the White River band; John Star (No. 18) and Tim Johnson (No. 16), both of whom are old warriors; Jim Pant (No. 22), whose early hunting was done with bow and arrows; Arkansaw (No. 23), a Paiute who has been among the Utes since his boyhood and is totally blind; Fanny Provo (No. 13), and Weeyutchee (No. 24). Six of the singers are members of the Uncompahgre band and live at Ouray. The oldest among these are Areev (No. 8), a man of strong character, who is leader among those opposing the introduction of mescal among the Utes in that locality. Allied with him in this position are Nikoree (No. 2), Jim Kolorow (No. 21), and Paul Pegaroos (No. 17). The younger members of the Uncompahgre band recording songs are Chigoop (No. 15) and Sidney Blueotter (No. 14). Among the singers of the White River and Uinta bands the following may be said to be in middle life: Mrs. Washington (No. 25), who treats the sick by material means; Teddy Pageets (No. 11), who treats the sick without the use of material means; Clark Tonner (No. 5); Isaacs (No. 4); Quinance (No. 7); and Dave Weetch (No. 19). Charlie Saritch is about the same age and was employed by the Government as policeman at the Whiterocks Boarding School in 1916, when the present work was concluded. To the younger generation belong Joshua Washington (No. 6), Andrew Frank (No. 12), and Eugene Perank (No. 10), whose surname is a mispronunciation of the English word "Frank."

Fred Mart (No. 3), who acted as the writer's interpreter throughout this research, was a student at the United States Indian School at Carlisle, Pa., 1903 to 1908. Charles Mack (No. 20) has been prominently identified with tribal affairs as an interpreter and has twice visited Washington with delegations.

GLOSSARY OF UTE WORDS

Tribal Names

The word "Ute" is of debated origin. The general term used by these Indians in referring to themselves or to others is Nönts, plural, Nöntši.

The three divisions of the tribe considered in the present work are:

(1) White River. This is a geographical term, the Ute name for this band being Ya'mpatika (yampa-eaters).[3]

---

[3] The yampa (*Carum gairdneri*) "is a plant whose roots are much used for food by the Indians of the Oregon region, the Klamath, Umatilla, Ute, and others; from *ya'mpä*, the name of this plant in the Ute dialect of Shoshonean." Handbook of American Indians, Bull. 30, Bur. Amer. Ethn., pt. 2, p. 987, Washington, 1910.

(2) Uinta, native name Uintaugump (*uinta*, at the edge; *ugump*, pine). This was said to refer to a dwelling place of this band, located where two mountain streams came together at an angle, making a point of land between the two streams. On this point of land was the lower edge of the pine timber, as it extended down from the mountain side. Thus the Uinta band were those who lived at the edge of the pine timber.

(3) Uncompahgre, native name Aŋkapagaritš, meaning "red lake" (*aŋagar*, red; *pagaritš*, lake).

NAMES OF CHIEFS

Tawatš, sun, commonly known as Tabby.
Nu'šina, origin and meaning unknown.

NAMES OF SINGERS

No. 1. To'pātšuk ("black otter"; *toka*, black; *pātšuk*, otter).

No. 2. Ni'kavari (*nika*, ear; *vari*, to hang down, to hang from).

No. 3. Native name not given.

No. 4. Magwitšint (said to refer to the act of wrapping a blanket around one's self).

No. 5. So'nawav (said to mean "God").

No. 6. Pa'tšatš, bat.

No. 7. Kwa'nantš, eagle

No. 8. Ariv, origin and meaning unknown.

No. 9. Sa'ritš, dog.

No. 10. Tavi'poniš (*tavi*, day, light; *ponis*, loosed, as something unbraided).

No. 11. Pa'gitš, little fish.

No. 12. See No. 10.

No. 13. Sato'yum ("white neck"; *sa*, white; *toyum*, neck).

No. 14. Sa'vapātšuk ("blue otter"; *sava*, blue; *pātšuk*, otter).

No. 15. Tšigu'p, a species of duck.

No. 16. Native name not given.

No. 17. Pegaru's, fine hair, or down.

No. 18. Sa'vawitopatš (blue dwarf-boy; *sava*, blue, *wito*, apparently referring to a dwarf; *apats*, boy).

No. 19. Witš, knife.

No. 20. Native name not given.

No. 21. Tšo'kwata'piyitš (Mexican chief; *tšo'kwa*, Mexican; *ta'piyitš*, chief).

No. 22. Pa'ant, tall.

No. 23. Kanav, willow.

No. 24. Wiyu'tš, awl (used as a needle).

No. 25. Sa'kwiagant ("white bear"; *sa*, white, *kwiagant*, bear).

WORDS OF SONGS

No. 1. *Áŋagar* (red), *vi'nuŋump* (descriptive term implying a rolling motion as of a wheel), *ku'avi'tšiya* (dust, derivation unknown), *ma'rikatš* (white man, from Spanish Americana; this term is generic and does not refer to an individual), *pumi'wanupahai* (looking around; the idea of the term is that of a man who pauses to look in all directions).

No. 2. *Oa'tšiwa'ones* (*oa*, yellow; the latter part said to mean hair sticking up).

No. 3. *Pāvi'tšu* (weasel skin), *puŋke* (hard, fast), *yamiko'vani* (swing, imperative verb).

No. 4. *Kwa'nantš* (eagle), *pututš* (down).

No. 40. *Tšiyuta* (said to be the term used by the Shoshoni in referring to these Indians, *tši* being a Shoshoni prefix).

No. 49. *To'kaneratš* (black sheep; *toka*, black; *kanerats*, sheep, from Spanish *carnero*).

No. 51. *Pinu'piya* (*pinu'*, most recent; *piya*, wife).

MUSICAL INSTRUMENTS

Morache, *woni'thokunap* (*woni*, standing; *thokunap*, rubbing the shorter stick upon the notched stick).

Drum, *pa'mpon*. This term is applied to both the small and large drums.

Flageolet, *wi'nip*.

Eagle bone whistle, carried in Sun dance, *gusau-ōka* (*gusau*, wing; *ōka*, whistle).

DANCES

Dance, *ni'tkap*.

Bear dance, *ma'makoni-ni'tkap* (*mamakoni*, said to refer to the step of the dance called a "reverse step, two forward and three backward").

Sun dance, *ta'vo-ni'tkap*.

Turkey dance (term applied by whites), *tho'nka-ni'tkap* (term applied by the Utes, meaning "jigging dance").

Women's dance, *ma'ma-ni'tkap*.

Lame dance, *sanku'-ni'tkap*.

Dragging-feet dance, *Tavi'yutšo'tavi-ni'tkap* (etymology unknown).

Tea dance, *ti'-ni'tkap* (*ti* is the English word "tea").

Double dance, *nawa'to-ni'tkap* (*nawa'to* is used with reference to anything that is doubled together).

Iron line dance, *pana'ka-tšuwi'ke-ni'tkap* (*pana'ka*, iron; *tšuwike*, line). The term is commonly abbreviated to *panatšuwi*.

General Terms

U'vwiuv, song; plural, *u'vwiuvi*.

Kovwiv, parade; *kovwiuv*, parade song.

Na'gokup, war; *na'gokup u'vwiuv*, war song.

Ni'a, hand-game.

Aviŋkwep, inclosure in which Bear dance is held.

Mutusukwi'gant, person who treats the sick by supernatural means, without administering herbs.

Bowa'gant, person who treats the sick by administering herbs.

NORTHERN UTE MUSIC

By Frances Densmore

THE UTE INDIANS [4]

TRIBAL NAME.—The word Ute is of disputed origin. In the early treaties with the United States Government and in reports of the Commissioner of Indian Affairs prior to the year 1859 the Indians now known as Utes were called Utahs.

HISTORY.—The Ute (or Utah) Indians formerly occupied the entire central and western portions of Colorado and the eastern part of Utah, including the eastern part of Salt Lake Valley and the Utah Valley. On the south they extended into New Mexico, occupying much of the upper drainage of the San Juan.[5] The first treaty between the Government of the United States and these Indians was proclaimed September 9, 1850.[6] The treaty opens thus:

"The following articles have been duly considered and solemnly adopted by the undersigned; that is to say, James S. Calhoun, Indian agent, residing at Santa Fe, acting commissioner on the part of the United States of America [here follow 26 names], principal and subordinate chiefs, representing the Utah tribe of Indians.

"I. The Utah tribe of Indians do hereby acknowledge and declare they are lawfully and exclusively under the jurisdiction of the Government of said States, and to its power and authority they now unconditionally submit."

A treaty with the Tabequache band of Utah Indians, proclaimed December 14, 1864,[7] indicates some progress on the part of these Indians, as it closes with the following clause: "The Government also agrees to establish and maintain a blacksmith shop and employ a competent blacksmith for the purpose of repairing the guns and agricultural implements which may be used by said Indians."

In 1868 a treaty was made with the "confederated bands of the Ute Nation" by which they received a large tract of land in the Ter-

---

[4] This description of the Ute Indians is intended to assist the reader in a sympathetic understanding of the material which follows, and should not be understood as offering exhaustive information on the several headings.

[5] Handbook of American Indians, Bull. 30, Bur. Amer. Ethn., pt. 2, pp. 874–876, Washington, 1910.

[6] Compilation of Treaties between the United States and the Indian Tribes. Washington, D. C., 1873, pp. 968–970.

[7] Ibid., pp. 970–974.

23

ritory of Colorado as their reservation.   In 1874, however, they relinquished a portion of this land, the agreement being made between "Felix R. Brunot, a commissioner in behalf of the United States, and the chiefs and people of the Tabequache, Muache, Capote, Weeminuche, Yampa, Grand River, and Uintah, the confederated bands of the Ute Nation."[8]   The first-named band is now known as the Uncompahgre.   A prominent chief of this period was known as Tabby.

A valley in northeastern Utah, comprising the present Uinta and Ouray Agency, was assigned to the Uinta band of Utes by proclamation of the President in 1861.[9]   There they were joined by the White River band in 1880, while the Uncompahgre and several other bands from the Colorado reservation agreed to settle on the La Plata River and on the Grand River near the mouth of the Gunnison.   Thus a majority of the Ute tribe were divided into 10 parts, which became known, respectively, as the Northern and Southern Utes.

Social organization.—Very little is known of the social organization of the tribe.   The writer was repeatedly informed by the oldest members of the tribe that the Utes had no societies, and that the only divisions of the tribe were bands, each led by a chief.

The Northern Utes.—The present work concerns only the Northern Utes, living on the Uinta and Ouray Reservation in northeastern Utah.   In addition to the Uinta and White River bands, located there by agreement, a considerable number of Uncompahgre are enrolled at that agency.   The Northern Utes have appeared in history chiefly through the journey away from the reservation, undertaken by the White River band.   The land on the Uinta Reservation was allotted in severalty in the year 1905.   The White River band objected to the restrictions this imposed upon them, and, failing in a protest, they decided to leave the reservation in a body. They started in the early summer of 1906 and went into Wyoming, apparently with the intention of going into the country of the Sioux. A diplomatic envoy, sent by the Commissioner of Indian Affairs, persuaded 45 of them to return.   The remainder were finally escorted to Fort Meade, S. Dak., by United States troops.   They went peacefully and were located on the Cheyenne River Reservation in South Dakota until June, 1908, when, at their own request, they were returned to the Uinta Reservation in Utah, reaching home in October of that year.   Red Cap, one of the two chiefs who led this expedition away from the reservation, was living when the material comprised in this book was collected and lent his influence to the furtherance of the work.

---

[8] Indian Laws and Treaties, compiled by Charles Kappler, Vol. I, pp. 151–152.   Washington, 1903.
[9] (Mentioned) ibid., p. 271.

HABITAT.—The Uinta and Ouray Reservation, where the material comprised in this book was collected, is located on a high plateau, north of which rise the Rocky Mountains (pl. 2, *a*, *b*). Sagebrush is the only native vegetation except along the courses of the rivers and streams that descend from the mountains (pl. 2, *c*, *d*). One of the canyons, known as White River Canyon (pl. 3, *a*), was the early home of the White River band. The Uinta band are scattered, their name, which undoubtedly was given them in some other locality, suggesting a preference for somewhat open country rather than the canyons. The members of the Uncompahgre band at the present time live about 30 miles south of the mountains along the Green River.

DWELLINGS.—Tipis covered with elk hide were said to be the early dwellings of the Utes, buffalo hide being used when it became available. Thatched dwellings were used by those too poor to have tipis and appear to have been commonly used by all the tribe during the summer. A dwelling of this type photographed by the writer (pl. 4, *a*) was identified by an officer of the United States Army as the type of dwelling which prevailed among the Utes in 1888, when he was stationed at Fort Duchesne. Log huts are extensively used as winter abodes at the present time, a typical summer camp being shown in plate 4, *b*.

TEMPERAMENT.—The Utes have never been a war-like tribe, yet they are a people of great tenacity of opinion. This has repeatedly brought them into difficulty with the Government. In contrast to this underlying tenacity, they seem characterized by quick transitions of mood concerning matters of less importance. These changing moods are like the brief, sudden storms that frequently occur in their native environment and are followed by sunshine.

LANGUAGE.—The Ute is a Shoshonean division of the Indian languages, related linguistically to the Paiute, Chemehuevi, Kawaiisu, and Bannock. It has not yet been studied intensively, but the following material on the subject is available for reference:

BARBER, A. E.—"Language and Utensils of the Modern Utes," U. S. Geological and Geographical Survey of the Territories, 1876, vol. 2, pp. 71–76.
CHAMBERLIN, RALPH V.—"Some Plant Names of the Ute Indians," American Anthropologist, vol. 2, No. 1, pp. 27–40.
HARRINGTON, JOHN P.—"The Phonetic System of the Ute Language," The University of Colorado Studies, vol. VIII, pp. 199–222, Pub. by Univ. of Col., Boulder, Colorado, 1910.
KROEBER, A. L.—"Notes on the Ute Language," American Anthropologist, vol. 10, pp. 74–87, 1908.

CLASSES OF SONGS.—The songs recorded among these people are chiefly those of social dances and of war, together with songs used in treating the sick. No attempt was made to enter on a detailed study of the Sun dance nor of an undetermined religious dance, around which there was placed a certain degree of mystery. The writer was informed that the Utes did not have songs to insure success in hunting, and no songs connected with hunting were offered for recording.

FOOD.—An old informant said: "When we lived farther east we ate berries, roots, and meat. We dried the meat of the deer, elk, and buffalo." Other native foods are piñon nuts, corn, and fish. The piñon nuts, even at the present time, are parched in hot ashes, after which the shells are removed and the nuts pounded on a stone. Corn is still ground by placing it on a broad, flat stone and rolling over it a rather long, round stone. The resultant meal is mixed with water and baked on heated earth, from which the ashes of a fire have been removed. According to Mason "the Ute Indians make use of many kinds of seeds in their dietary," [9] gathering them on the plains.

INDUSTRIES.—Pottery was made by the ancient Utes, but the basket bottle with inner coating of pitch is now in general use. The basketry of the Utes is designed for utility and includes gathering and carrying baskets, trays, bowls, harvesting fans, and women's hats.[10]

COMPOSITION OF SONGS.—It was said by several singers that they "heard a song in their sleep," sang it, and either awoke to find themselves singing it aloud or remembered it and were able to sing it. No information was obtained on any other method of producing songs. In this connection the writer desires to record an observation on musical composition among the Sioux. A song was sung at a gathering and she remarked: "That is different from any Sioux song I have heard, it has so *many* peculiarities." The interpreter replied, "That song was composed recently by several men working together. Each man suggested something, and they put it all together in the song." This is the only instance of cooperation in the composition of an Indian song that has been observed.

MUSICAL INSTRUMENTS.—The dance songs and war songs of the Utes are accompanied by the morache, hand drum, and large drum, while the hand game songs are accompanied by beating on a horizontal pole, and certain songs of the camp were formerly accompanied by beating on a stiff rawhide.

Morache.—This instrument is used to accompany the songs of the Bear dance (pp. 58–72). The instrument in various forms has been noted among many tribes of Indians, and the Spanish term *morache* has become established by usage. It is, however, classified as a "notched stick rattle with resonator" by Mr. E. H. Hawley, curator of musical instruments, United States National Museum, Washington, D. C. The instrument comprises three units: (1) A

---

[9] Mason, Otis T. Indian Basketry, vol. 2, p. 439, London, 1905.
[10] Ibid., vol. 1, pp. 71–72; vol. 2, pp. 434–441.

a, Looking north

b, Looking south

c, Uinta River

d, Rock formation near Uinta River

PLATEAU OF UINTA AND OURAY RESERVATION

a, White River Canyon

b, Burial place in vicinity of White River Canyon

a, Entrance to thatched dwelling

b, Summer camp

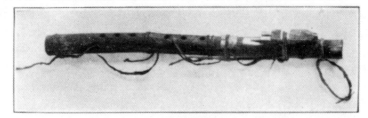

a, Flageolet

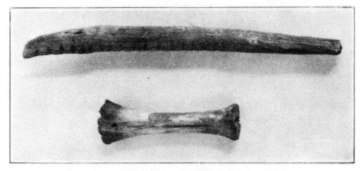

b, Notched stick (shaped like jawbone of bear) with bone "rubber"

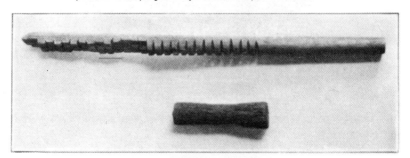

c, Notched stick (straight) with rubbing stick

d, Basket resonator

stick in which notches are cut; (2) a short stick (or bone) rubbed across these notches; and (3) a resonator placed over a hole in the ground. This resonator was formerly a shallow basket (pl. 5, *d*), but in recent times a piece of zinc is used. The end of the longer stick is rested on the resonator, while the shorter stick is rubbed perpendicularly, the downward stroke being sharply accented (pl. 1). Two specimens of the notched stick and the rubbing stick were obtained by the writer, both sets having been used in the Bear dance on the Uinta and Ouray Reservations (pl. 5, *b*, *c*). The more typical of these comprises a notched stick shaped like the jawbone of a bear, with a bone for rubbing stick.[10] The other set comprises a straight stick, in which notches have been cut, and a smaller stick for rubbing across it. This set, with the basket resonator, is described as follows by Mr. Hawley:

"Name of specimen, Notched Stick Rattle. Notched stick, L. 25⅛ in., diameter 1¼ in. Rubbing stick, L. 6 in., diameter 1¾ in. Basket resonator, H. 5 in., diameter 15¾ in. The notched stick originally had 28 notches about ¾ of an inch deep made in 20¾ inches. On the opposite side 24 more shallow notches were cut in a space of 12 inches. The rubber is oval in cross-section, rubbing across the notches having reduced the diameter to 1 5/16 in. The resonator is of a shallow hemispherical form. It is not a drum. It is not put in vibration by being beaten or frictioned. A hole is dug in the ground and the basket is inverted over the hole. One end of the notched stick rests on the basket. The vibrations of the notched stick are communicated to the basket, which in turn so sets in vibration the air confined in the hole and basket as to dominate the original vibration."

The Pima Indians, according to Frank Russell, use the "basket-drum" and "scraping sticks" separately as well as in combination. Mr. Russell says: "Any shallow basket of sufficient size, such as are in common use in every household for containing grain or prepared food, may be transformed into a drum by simply turning it bottom up and beating it with the hands. In accompanying certain songs it is struck with a stick in rapid, glancing blows. The notched or scraping stick is in very general use to carry the rhythm during the singing of ceremonial songs. When one end of the stick is laid on an overturned basket and another stick or a deer's scapula is drawn quickly over the notches, the resulting sound from this compound instrument of percussion may be compared to that of the snare drum. However, it is usually held in the hand and rasped with a small stick kept for the purpose. So important are these

---

[10] "Among the negroes of the Southern States the jawbone of a mule or horse is used in the same way, a stick being rubbed over the teeth." Catalogue of the Crosby-Brown Collection of Musical Instruments, published by the Metropolitan Museum of Art, New York, 1914, footnote, p. 183.

instruments in Pima rain ceremonies that they are usually spoken of as "rain sticks."[11] Serrated instruments, with rasping sticks, were also used by the Negroes of central Africa and by the Chinese.

Hand drum.—This instrument is used with songs of the Lame dance (pp. 105–111), Double dance (pp. 118–119), and Iron-line dance (p. 120), as well as with war songs (pp. 146–160) and parade songs (pp. 166–173). A specimen of the hand drum (pl. 6) was obtained and is described as follows by Mr. Hawley: "Small drum. H. 3⅝ in., dia. 12¾ in. Shell of bent wood, the joint lapped and nailed. The inside is reinforced with a strip of bent wood 1¼ in. wide, $\frac{3}{16}$ in. thick; its ends do not quite meet; one skin head stretched over the shell when wet. It extends halfway down the outside of the shell. Holes are made in the edge of the skin 1⅜ in. apart, also corresponding holes in the median line of the shell and its reinforcement. Two buckskin thongs are passed in and out through these holes in opposite directions and tied inside. A handle of two strips of cotton cloth cross each other at right angles. A handhold is formed by bringing these together for about 1¼ inches at the center and wrapping them with a strip of cloth (pl. 7). Near one end of the reinforcement a buckskin loop to suspend it is attached to the thong that binds the skin head to the shell. Both outside and inside have been colored yellow. The skin is so heavy that its shrinkage has misshaped the shell. Drumstick, handle, a round stick like a section of a grapevine. Head of white cotton cloth wrapped several times around one end of stick, held by tying its ends together. Stick, L. 12½ in., dia. $\frac{7}{16}$ in.; head, L. 4¼ in., dia. 1¼ inches."

Large drum.—It is interesting to note that the large drum is used with the Turkey dance and Woman's dance, the former, and probably the latter, of these dances being introduced among the Utes from other tribes. This drum is of the usual type and is placed on the ground, the singers sitting around it and drumming as they sing. The usual size permits the seating of 8 or 10 drummers around it, but it is said that 14 men are sometimes seated at a drum.

Flageolet.—In general construction this instrument (pl. 5, *a*) resembles the flageolet used in many other tribes. It is made of a straight section of wood which has been split lengthwise, the pith removed, and the two pieces glued together. In length it is about 11 inches and in diameter 1⅛ inches. It has a whistle mouthpiece with the windway outside. The sound holes are in two groups of three each, those in the group farthest from the mouthpiece being slightly nearer together than those in the other group. The instrument was played for the writer, and had an extended range and a pleasing quality of tone. It is said that a much better tone is produced if the instru-

---

[11] Russell, Frank, The Pima Indians. Twenty-sixth Ann. Rept. Bur. Amer. Ethn., p. 167, Washington, 1908.

a, Obverse

b, Reverse

HAND DRUM WITH DRUMMING STICK

UTE BEATING HAND DRUM

ment is moistened. A member of the Ute tribe who made and played on such a flageolet said: "American song tunes can not be played on it but Indian music can be played on it."

NOTES ON BURIAL CUSTOMS.--Cave burial was formerly practiced by the Utes. It is said that "Ouray, the Ute chief, . . . was buried, so far as could be ascertained, in a rock fissure or cave." [12] Instances of cave burial are also recorded.[13] A burial ground was visited by the writer which appeared to be still in use. On the burial places were the bones of horses and dogs which, it was said, had been slain at the death of their owners. Clothing was hung above the graves, and, in one instance, a quantity of corn was suspended from the branch of a tree (pl. 3, *b*).

---

[12] Yarrow, H. C. A further Contribution to the Mortuary Customs of the North American Indians. First Rept. Bur. Amer. Ethn., p. 128, Washington, 1881.

[13] Ibid., p. 142.

TABULATED ANALYSIS OF CHIPPEWA, SIOUX, AND UTE SONGS

MELODIC ANALYSIS

TABLE 1.—TONALITY [1]

	Bear dance songs	Sun dance and undetermined dance songs	Social dance songs	Songs used in treatment of sick	War songs	Hand game songs	Parade and miscellaneous songs	Ute songs Number	Ute songs Per cent	Chippewa and Sioux songs [2] Number	Chippewa and Sioux songs [2] Per cent	Chippewa, Sioux, and Ute songs Number	Chippewa, Sioux, and Ute songs Per cent
Major tonality	12	6	16	10	11	7	16	78	71	299	50	377	53
Minor tonality	5	6	4	1	5		3	24	22	296	49	320	45
Third lacking			2	4		2		8	7			8	1
Beginning major, ending minor										2		2	
Beginning minor, ending major										1		1	
Irregular										2		2	
Total	17	12	22	15	16	9	19	110		600		710	

TABLE 2.—FIRST NOTE OF SONG—ITS RELATION TO KEYNOTE

Beginning on the—	Bear dance songs	Sun dance and undetermined dance songs	Social dance songs	Songs used in treatment of sick	War songs	Hand game songs	Parade and miscellaneous songs	Ute songs Number	Ute songs Per cent	Chippewa and Sioux songs[2] Number	Chippewa and Sioux songs[2] Per cent	Chippewa, Sioux, and Ute songs Number	Chippewa, Sioux, and Ute songs Per cent
Fourteenth										1		1	
Thirteenth										4	1	4	1
Twelfth		2	1				1	4	3	135	23	139	20
Eleventh					1			1	1	11	2	12	2
Tenth			2					2	2	49	8	51	7
Ninth			1				2	3	3	25	4	28	4
Octave	2	3	9	1	9	3	4	31	28	123	21	154	22
Seventh	1							1	1	8	1	9	1
Sixth	1			1	1			3	3	13	2	16	2
Fifth	3	6	3	8	4	2	8	34	31	144	24	178	25
Fourth				1	1			2	2	10	1	12	1
Third	8	1	2			3	3	17	15	30	5	47	7
Second	1		1	1				3	3	12	2	15	2
Keynote	1		3	3		1	1	9	8	33	5	42	6
Irregular										2		2	
Total	17	12	22	15	16	9	19	110		600		710	

[1] Since we are considering the music of a people among whom scales and keys were not formulated, the terms "major tonality" and "minor tonality" are used in preference to "major key" and "minor key." Tonality is defined as "the quality and peculiarity of a tonal system" and key as "a system of tones the members of which bear definite relations to each other."

[2] See Bulletin 61, pp 26–39.

TABULATED ANALYSIS OF CHIPPEWA, SIOUX, AND UTE SONGS—Continued

MELODIC ANALYSIS—continued

TABLE 3.—LAST NOTE OF SONG—ITS RELATION TO KEYNOTE

Ending on the—	Bear dance songs	Sun dance and undetermined dance songs	Social dance songs	Songs used in treatment of sick	War songs	Hand game songs	Parade and miscellaneous songs	Ute songs		Chippewa and Sioux songs		Chippewa, Sioux, and Ute songs	
								Number	Per cent	Number	Per cent	Number	Per cent
Fifth	6	7	11	7	3	2	11	47	43	155	26	202	28
Third	1		4		2	1		8	7	72	12	80	11
Keynote	10	5	7	8	11	6	8	55	50	371	62	426	60
Irregular										2		2	
Total	17	12	22	15	16	9	19	110		600		710	

TABLE 4.—LAST NOTE OF SONG—ITS RELATION TO COMPASS OF SONG

	Bear dance songs	Sun dance and undetermined dance songs	Social dance songs	Songs used in treatment of sick	War songs	Hand game songs	Parade and miscellaneous songs	Ute songs Number	Ute songs Per cent	Chippewa and Sioux songs Number	Chippewa and Sioux songs Per cent	Chippewa, Sioux, and Ute songs Number	Chippewa, Sioux, and Ute songs Per cent
Songs in which final tone is—													
Lowest tone in song	7	10	14	12	12	6	16	77	70	537	90	616	87
Highest tone in song										1		1	
Immediately preceded by—													
Fifth below										1		1	
Fourth below	3							3	3	9	1	12	2
Major third below			1					1	1	3		4	
Minor third below	1		1		2			5	4	9	1	14	2
Whole tone below	1		3			1		5	4	12	2	17	2
Semitone below	1						1	2	2	3		5	1
Whole tone below with sixth below in a previous measure	1							1	1			1	
Whole tone below with fourth below in a previous measure	1			3	1	1		6	5	1		7	1
Whole tone below with minor third below in a previous measure							1	1	1			1	
Songs containing a fourth below the final tone					1			1	1	7	1	8	1
Songs containing a major third below the final tone			1					2	2	4		6	1
Songs containing a minor third below the final tone	1	1	1					4	4	10	2	14	2
Songs containing a whole tone below the final tone	1	1				1	1			2		2	
Songs containing a semitone below the final tone										1		1	
Total	17	12	22	15	16	9	19	110		600		710	

TABULATED ANALYSIS OF CHIPPEWA, SIOUX, AND UTE SONGS—Continued

MELODIC ANALYSIS—continued

TABLE 5.—NUMBER OF TONES COMPRISING COMPASS OF SONG

Compass of—	Bear dance songs	Sun dance and undetermined dance songs	Social dance songs	Songs used in treatment of sick	War songs	Hand game songs	Parade and miscellaneous songs	Ute songs		Chippewa and Sioux songs		Chippewa, Sioux, and Ute songs	
								Number	Per cent	Number	Per cent	Number	Per cent
Seventeen tones										3		3	
Fifteen tones			1					1	1			1	
Fourteen tones										14	2	14	2
Thirteen tones		1	1					2	2	46	8	48	7
Twelve tones		3	3		1		3	10	9	147	25	157	22
Eleven tones	1		6		1		2	10	9	45	8	55	8
Ten tones		1	3	2	2		2	10	9	81	14	91	13
Nine tones	4	2	3	1	4	2	2	18	16	51	9	69	10
Eight tones	6	5	2	5	8	1	7	34	31	156	26	190	27
Seven tones	4		1	5			1	7	6	20	3	27	4
Six tones	4		1	2		3	2	12	11	19	3	31	4
Five tones	1					2		3	3	14	2	17	2
Four tones	1							1	1	4	1	5	1
Three tones			1			1		2	2			2	
Total	17	12	22	15	16	9	19	110		600		710	

TABLE 6.—TONE MATERIAL

	Bear dance songs	Sun dance and undetermined dance songs	Social dance songs	Songs used in treatment of sick	War songs	Hand game songs	Parade and miscellaneous songs	Ute songs		Chippewa and Sioux songs		Chippewa, Sioux, and Ute songs	
								Number	Per cent	Number	Per cent	Number	Per cent
First five-toned scale										2		2	
Second five-toned scale	1	1	2		2		1	7	6	74	12	81	11
Fourth five-toned scale	3		4	3	6	1	3	20	18	137	23	157	22
Fifth five-toned scale										2		2	
Major triad	2				1	2		5	5	5	1	10	1
Major triad and seventh						1		1	1	2		3	
Major triad and sixth	2		1		2			5	5	46	8	51	7
Major triad and fourth	2						1	3	3	2		5	1
Major triad and second	1		3	6	1	2	4	17	15	11	2	28	4
Minor triad										3		3	
Minor triad and seventh	1				1			2	2	4	1	6	1
Minor triad and sixth										6	1	6	1
Minor triad and fourth		1	1	1	1			4	4	49	8	53	8
Minor triad and second										2		2	
Octave complete	1	3	2				1	7	6	35	6	42	6
Octave complete except seventh	1	3	3				5	12	11	54	9	66	9
Octave complete except seventh and sixth		1	1	1	1		1	5	6	22	4	27	4
Octave complete except seventh, sixth, and fourth										1		1	
Octave complete except seventh, fifth, and second										1		1	
Octave complete except seventh and fourth [1]										9	1	9	1
Octave complete except seventh and third			1					1	1	2		3	
Octave complete except seventh and second	2		1					3	3	21	4	24	3
Octave complete except sixth										29	5	29	4

[1] These songs are minor in tonality, the mediant being a minor third above the tonic and the submediant a minor sixth above the tonic. In the fourth five-toned scale the seventh and fourth tones are also omitted, but the corresponding intervals are major and the songs are major in tonality.

TABULATED ANALYSIS OF CHIPPEWA, SIOUX, AND UTE SONGS—Continued

MELODIC ANALYSIS—continued

TABLE 6—TONE MATERIAL—Continued

	Bear dance songs	Sun dance and undetermined dance songs	Social dance songs	Songs used in treatment of sick	War songs	Hand game songs	Parade and miscellaneous songs	Ute songs		Chippewa and Sioux songs		Chippewa, Sioux, and Ute songs	
								Number	Per cent	Number	Per cent	Number	Per cent
Octave complete except sixth and fifth										1		1	
Octave complete except sixth and fourth	1							1	1	3	1	4	1
Octave complete except sixth and third										1		1	
Octave complete except sixth and second										5	1	5	1
Octave complete except sixth, fifth, and second										2		2	
Octave complete except fifth and second			1					1	1			1	
Octave complete except fourth		1					1	3	3	15	2	18	3
Octave complete except fourth and third										1		1	
Octave complete except fourth and second										4	1	4	1
Octave complete except third			1					1	1	1		2	
Octave complete except third and second		1						1	1			1	
Octave complete except second								1	1	21	4	22	3
Minor third and seventh	1							1	1			1	1
Minor third and fourth	1		1		1			1	1	4	1	5	1
Minor third, seventh, and fourth								2	2			2	2
First, fourth, and fifth tones						1		1	1	1		1	
First, second, and fifth tones										1		1	
First, second, fourth, and fifth tones						1		2	2	1		3	
First, second, fifth, and sixth tones				1		1		4	4	6	1	10	1
First, second, third, and sixth tones				3		1	1	1	1	12	2	13	2
Total	17	12	22	15	16	9	19	110		600		710	

TABLE 7.—ACCIDENTALS [1]

Songs containing—	Bear dance songs	Sun dance and undetermined dance songs	Social dance songs	Songs used in treatment of sick	War songs	Hand game songs	Parade and miscellaneous songs	Ute songs Number	Ute songs Per cent	Chippewa and Sioux songs Number	Chippewa and Sioux songs Per cent	Chippewa, Sioux, and Ute songs Number	Chippewa, Sioux, and Ute songs Per cent
No accidentals	16	12	22	15	15	9	17	106	96	502	84	608	86
Seventh raised a semitone							1	1	1	15	2	16	2
Sixth raised a semitone										13	2	13	2
Fourth raised a semitone	1				1		1	3	3	8	1	11	2
Third raised a semitone										1		1	
Second raised a semitone										6	1	6	1
Seventh lowered a semitone										4	1	4	1
Sixth lowered a semitone										21	4	21	3
Fifth lowered a semitone										1		1	
Fourth lowered a semitone										5	1	5	1
Third lowered a semitone										6	1	6	1
Second lowered a semitone										8	1	8	1
Seventh and fourth raised a semitone										2		2	
Sixth and third raised a semitone										1		1	
Fourth raised a semitone and second lowered a semitone										1		1	
Second raised a semitone and sixth lowered a semitone										1		1	
Fourth raised a semitone and third and second lowered a semitone										1		1	
Seventh and fourth lowered a semitone										1		1	
Second, third, and sixth lowered a semitone										1		1	
Irregular										2		2	
Total	17	12	22	15	16	9	19	110		600		710	

[1] Students desiring to observe the accidentals with reference to the tonality of the songs are referred to the tables at the conclusion of the several groups of songs, in which the serial numbers of the songs are given.

TABULATED ANALYSIS OF CHIPPEWA, SIOUX, AND UTE SONGS—Continued

MELODIC ANALYSIS—continued

TABLE 8.—STRUCTURE

	Bear dance songs	Sun dance and undetermined dance songs	Social dance songs	Songs used in treatment of sick	War songs	Hand game songs	Parade and miscellaneous songs	Ute songs		Chippewa and Sioux songs		Chippewa, Sioux, and Ute songs	
								Number	Per cent	Number	Per cent	Number	Per cent
Melodic [1]	8	3	11	11	8	4	9	54	49	397	66	451	64
Melodic with harmonic framework [2]	5	8	3	4	6		6	32	29	85	14	117	16
Harmonic [3]	4	1	8		2	5	4	24	22	116	19	140	20
Irregular								2		2		2	
Total	17	12	22	15	16	9	19	110		600		710	

TABLE 9.—FIRST PROGRESSION—DOWNWARD AND UPWARD

	Bear dance songs	Sun dance and undetermined dance songs	Social dance songs	Songs used in treatment of sick	War songs	Hand game songs	Parade and miscellaneous songs	Ute songs		Chippewa and Sioux songs		Chippewa, Sioux, and Ute songs	
								Number	Per cent	Number	Per cent	Number	Per cent
Downward	15	8	14	5	14	6	14	76	69	415	69	491	69
Upward	2	4	8	10	2	3	5	34	31	185	31	219	31
Total	17	12	22	15	16	9	19	110		600		710	

TABLE 10.—TOTAL NUMBER OF PROGRESSIONS—DOWNWARD AND UPWARD

	Bear dance songs	Sun dance and undetermined dance songs	Social dance songs	Songs used in treatment of sick	War songs	Hand game songs	Parade and miscellaneous songs	Ute songs		Chippewa and Sioux songs		Chippewa, Sioux, and Ute songs	
								Number	Per cent	Number	Per cent	Number	Per cent
Downward	283	224	420	209	285	127	339	1,887	61	10,419	64	12,306	64
Upward	209	133	248	151	175	96	214	1,226	39	5,736	36	6,962	36
Total	492	357	668	360	460	223	553	3,113		16,155		19,268	

[1] Songs are thus classified if contiguous accented tones do not bear a simple chord-relation to each other.

[2] Songs are thus classified if only a portion of the contiguous accented tones bear a chord-relation to each other.

[3] Songs are thus classified if contiguous accented tones bear a simple chord-relation to each other.

TABULATED ANALYSIS OF CHIPPEWA, SIOUX, AND UTE SONGS—Continued

MELODIC ANALYSIS—continued

TABLE 11.—INTERVALS IN DOWNWARD PROGRESSION

Interval of a—	Bear dance songs	Sun dance and undetermined dance songs	Social dance songs	Songs used in treatment of sick	War songs	Hand game songs	Parade and miscellaneous songs	Ute songs — Number	Ute songs — Per cent	Chippewa and Sioux songs — Number	Chippewa and Sioux songs — Per cent	Chippewa, Sioux, and Ute songs — Number	Chippewa, Sioux, and Ute songs — Per cent
Twelfth										1		1	
Ninth										1		1	
Octave										2		2	
Seventh										2		2	
Major sixth										13		13	
Minor sixth	3	3		2	1			9		6		15	
Fifth	5	3		1	16	1	4	30	*2*	88	*1*	118	*1*
Fourth	46	23	50	40	38	20	64	281	*15*	968	*9*	1,249	*10*
Major third	95	14	29	9	31	30	35	243	*13*	975	*9*	1,218	*10*
Minor third	57	53	140	29	83	29	55	446	*24*	3,334	*32*	3,780	*31*
Augmented second										6		6	
Major second	69	113	190	127	110	45	170	824	*44*	4,755	*46*	5,579	*45*
Minor second	8	15	11	1	6	2	11	54	*3*	268		322	
Total	283	224	420	209	285	127	339	1,887		10,419		12,306	

TABLE 12.—INTERVALS IN UPWARD PROGRESSION

Interval of a—	Bear dance songs	Sun dance and undetermined dance songs	Social dance songs	Songs used in treatment of sick	War songs	Hand game songs	Parade and miscellaneous songs	Ute songs		Chippewa and Sioux songs		Chippewa, Sioux, and Ute songs	
								Number	Per cent	Number	Per cent	Number	Per cent
Fourteenth										1		1	
Twelfth										17		17	
Eleventh										4		4	
Tenth										11		11	
Ninth	1		1		1		1	4		10		14	
Octave	2	3	3		3		1	12	1	108	2	120	2
Seventh	1		1		1		1	4		22		26	
Major sixth	1	2	2	2	3		2	12	1	64	1	76	1
Minor sixth	4	3	6	3	4		2	22	2	33	1	55	1
Fifth	10	6	10	9	26	5	23	89	7	358	6	447	6
Fourth	36	22	35	22	24	17	42	198	16	841	15	1,039	15
Major third	69	14	26	9	10	21	22	171	14	625	11	796	11
Minor third	40	26	78	13	52	16	21	246	20	1,561	27	1,807	26
Major second	39	50	84	92	46	35	93	439	36	1,912	33	2,351	34
Minor second	6	7	2	1	5	2	6	29	2	169	3	198	3
Total	209	133	248	151	175	96	214	1,226		5,736		6,962	

TABULATED ANALYSIS OF CHIPPEWA, SIOUX, AND UTE SONGS—Continued

MELODIC ANALYSIS—continued

TABLE 13.—AVERAGE NUMBER OF SEMITONES IN EACH INTERVAL

	Bear dance songs	Sun dance and undetermined dance songs	Social dance songs	Songs used in treatment of sick	War songs	Hand game songs	Parade and miscellaneous songs	Total of Ute songs	Total of Chippewa and Sioux songs	Total of Chippewa, Sioux, and Ute songs
Number of intervals	492	357	668	360	460	223	553	3,113	16,155	19,268
Number of semitones	1,805	1,095	1,657	1,076	1,625	730	1,789	9,777	48,805	58,582
Average number of semitones in an interval	3.6	3.06	2.4	2.9	3.5	3.2	3	3.14	3.02	3.04

TABLE 14.—KEY [1]

	Bear dance songs	Sun dance and undetermined dance songs	Social dance songs	Songs used in treatment of sick	War songs	Hand game songs	Parade and miscellaneous songs	Ute songs		Chippewa and Sioux songs		Chippewa, Sioux, and Ute songs	
								Number	Per cent	Number	Per cent	Number	Per cent
Key of—													
A major	2	1						7	6	31	5	38	5
A minor		1				1		1	1	36	6	37	5
B flat major	2	1	2	2				8	7	30	5	38	5
B flat minor		3		1			1	6	5	17	3	23	3
B major			3		1			4	4	18	3	22	3
B minor		1	1					1	1	34	6	35	5
C major	1			2				7	6	21	4	28	4
C minor	2	1					3	3	3	28	5	31	4

Key										
D flat major	31	24					1	1		2
C sharp minor	19	19		2						1
D major	24	19	5	2	1	1			1	1
D minor	28	28		2	1					1
E flat major	26	17	8							
E flat minor	28	27	1	2				7		
E major	24	14	9		1					
E minor	13	13		2		1				
F major	40	38	2	2						1
F minor	25	24	1			2				
G flat major	30	27	3	1						1
F sharp major	1	1								
F sharp minor	19	17	2	1	2		3	1	2	2
G major	60	49	11	1					2	2
G minor	30	28	2						1	1
A flat major	26	21	5	2	1	1				
G sharp minor	21	14	7	1	2	2	2	2	1	
Third lacking	8		8							
Beginning major, ending minor	2	2								
Beginning minor, ending major	1	1								
Irregular	2	2								
Total	710	600	110	19	9	16	15	22	12	17

¹ The word "key" is here used in its broad sense, as applicable to non-harmonic music, inclusive of modes.

TABULATED ANALYSIS OF CHIPPEWA, SIOUX, AND UTE SONGS—Continued

RHYTHMIC ANALYSIS

TABLE 15.—PART OF MEASURE ON WHICH SONG BEGINS

	Bear dance songs	Sun dance and undetermined dance songs	Social dance songs	Songs used in treatment of sick	War songs	Hand game songs	Parade and miscellaneous songs	Ute songs Number	Ute songs Per cent	Chippewa and Sioux songs Number	Chippewa and Sioux songs Per cent	Chippewa, Sioux, and Ute songs Number	Chippewa, Sioux, and Ute songs Per cent
Beginning on unaccented part of measure	5	2	6	3	3	3	3	25	23	217	39	242	36
Beginning on accented part of measure	12	10	16	12	13	6	16	85	76	341	61	426	64
Transcribed in outline[1]										42		42	
Total	17	12	22	15	16	9	19	110		600		710	

TABLE 16.—RHYTHM (METER) OF FIRST MEASURE

	Bear dance songs	Sun dance and undetermined dance songs	Social dance songs	Songs used in treatment of sick	War songs	Hand game songs	Parade and miscellaneous songs	Ute songs Number	Ute songs Per cent	Chippewa and Sioux songs Number	Chippewa and Sioux songs Per cent	Chippewa, Sioux, and Ute songs Number	Chippewa, Sioux, and Ute songs Per cent
First measure in—													
2-4 time	11	6	13	12	9	5	12	68	62	300	54	368	55
3-4 time	6	5	9	3	5	4	7	39	35	220	39	259	39
4-4 time										9	2	9	1
5-4 time										13	2	13	2
6-4 time										1		1	

	Ute songs		Chippewa and Sioux songs		Chippewa, Sioux, and Ute songs	
	Number	Per cent	Number	Per cent	Number	Per cent
7-4 time			2		2	
3-8 time			4	*1*	4	*1*
4-8 time	2	*2*	3	*1*	5	*1*
5-8 time	1	*1*	4	*1*	5	*1*
2-2 time			2		2	
Transcribed in outline¹			42		42	
Total	110		600		710	

TABLE 17.—CHANGE OF TIME, MEASURE LENGTHS

	Bear dance songs	Sun dance and undetermined dance songs	Social dance songs	Songs used in treatment of sick	War songs	Hand game songs	Parade and miscellaneous songs	Ute songs		Chippewa and Sioux songs		Chippewa, Sioux, and Ute songs	
								Number	Per cent	Number	Per cent	Number	Per cent
Songs containing no change of time	4	2	3		1	2		12	*11*	88	*16*	100	*15*
Songs containing a change of time	13	10	19	15	15	7	19	98	*89*	470	*84*	568	*85*
Transcribed in outline¹										42		42	
Total	17	12	22	15	16	9	19	110		600		710	

¹ Excluded in computing percentage.

TABULATED ANALYSIS OF CHIPPEWA, SIOUX, AND UTE SONGS—Continued

RHYTHMIC ANALYSIS—continued

TABLE 18.—RHYTHM (METER) OF DRUM OR MORACHE

	Bear dance songs	Sun dance and undetermined dance songs	Social dance songs	Songs used in treatment of sick	War songs	Hand game songs	Parade and miscellaneous songs	Ute songs		Chippewa and Sioux songs		Chippewa, Sioux, and Ute songs	
								Number	Per cent	Number	Per cent	Number	Per cent
Sixteenth notes unaccented [1]						1		1	2	1		2	
Eighth notes accented in groups of two										21	6	21	5
Eighth notes unaccented [2]		5	7		3	5	3	23	36	143	39	166	39
Quarter notes unaccented [3]	10	1	8		5		6	30	46	56	15	86	20
Half notes unaccented										5	1	5	1
Each accented beat preceded by an unaccented beat corresponding approximately to the third count of a triplet [4]			5					5	8	124	34	129	30
Each accented beat followed by an unaccented beat corresponding approximately to the second count of a triplet [5]							2	2	3	2	1	4	1
Each accented beat preceded by an unaccented beat corresponding to the fourth member of a group of four sixteenth notes													
Tremolo drumbeat in opening measures, followed by drumbeat in quarter-note values [6]		6	2	15	1		3	4	6	14	4	14	3
Drum not recorded [7]	7				7	3	5	45		234		279	
Total	17	12	22	15	16	9	19	110		600		710	

[1] See No. 100. [2] See No. 18. [3] See Nos. 2 and 20. [4] See No. 36. [5] See No. 108. [6] See No. 72. [7] Excluded in computing percentage.

TABLE 19.—RHYTHMIC UNIT¹ OF SONG

Songs containing—	Bear dance songs	Sun dance and undetermined dance songs	Social dance songs	Songs used in treatment of sick	War songs	Hand game songs	Parade and miscellaneous songs	Ute songs		Chippewa and Sioux songs		Chippewa, Sioux, and Ute songs	
								Number	Per cent	Number	Per cent	Number	Per cent
No rhythmic unit	2	4	5	1	1	3	11	27	25	185	33	212	32
One rhythmic unit	9	4	12	12	11	6	6	60	55	335	60	395	59
Two rhythmic units	6	4	3	2	4		1	20	18	32	6	52	8
Three rhythmic units			2					3	3	4	1	7	1
Four rhythmic units										1		1	
Five rhythmic units												1	
Transcribed in outline²										42		42	
Total	17	12	22	15	16	9	19	110		600		710	

¹ The word "unit" is here used in accordance with the first definition given by the Century Dictionary—"Unit. Any one of the individuals or similar groups into which a complex whole can be analyzed."
² Excluded in computing percentage.

TABULATED ANALYSIS OF CHIPPEWA, SIOUX, AND UTE SONGS—Continued

RHYTHMIC ANALYSIS—continued

TABLE 20.—TIME UNIT[1] OF VOICE (AT BEGINNING OF SONG)

Metronome	Bear dance songs	Sun dance and undetermined dance songs	Social dance songs	Songs used in treatment of sick	War songs	Hand game songs	Parade and miscellaneous songs	Ute songs Number	Ute songs Per cent	Chippewa and Sioux songs Number	Chippewa and Sioux songs Per cent	Chippewa, Sioux, and Ute songs Number	Chippewa, Sioux, and Ute songs Per cent
44										1		1	
48										1		1	
50										1		1	
52										5	1	5	1
54										5	1	5	1
56										4	1	4	1
58	1			9				10	9	5	1	15	2
60					1	1	1	3	3	18	3	21	3
63	2		1	1	1		2	8	7	16	3	24	4
66	1			1	3		4	9	8	21	4	30	4
69		1	1		1			3	3	18	3	21	3
72	1	3	1		1			8	7	31	5	30	4
76	1	1	3	2	1		3	9	8	32	5	41	6
80			4		1			7	6	35	6	40	6
84		2	1		2		2	6	5	32	5	38	6
88		2	1	1	1		1	5	5	38	6	36	5
92	1	1	1	1	1	1		6	5	37	5	44	7
96			1			1	1	4	4	29	5	41	6
100						1	1	1	1	28	4	30	4
104	4	1	5		1	1		12	11	28	5	40	6
108	1		1			1		2	2	24	4	26	4

M. M.								Total	Number	Per cent	Number	Per cent
112			1			1			23	4	25	4
116			1						15	3	15	8
120	1						2		16	3	20	8
126	1			1	2				11	2	14	1
132		1				1	2		7	1	10	1
138									4	2	4	2
144	2								12	1	14	1
152									5	2	5	2
160				1	1				12	3	12	3
168									16	1	17	1
176									8	1	8	1
184									5	1	5	1
192									6	1	6	1
200									6		6	
208									2		2	
Rubato									2		2	
Transcribed in outline²									42		42	
Total	17	12	22	15	16	9	19	110	600		710	

¹ In this work the term "time unit" is substituted for "metric unit," which was used in the analyses of Chippewa and Sioux songs. In a majority of transcriptions the time unit is a quarter note. The duration of this time unit is determined by the beat of a Maelzel metronome, the numbers in this table corresponding to those on the pendulum of the metronome and indicating, respectively, the number of beats per minute. The word "unit" is here used in accordance with the second definition given by the Century Dictionary— "Unit. Any standard quantity by the repetition of which, or of some subdivision of it, any other quantity of the same kind is measured."

² Excluded in computing percentage.

TABULATED ANALYSIS OF CHIPPEWA, SIOUX, AND UTE SONGS—Continued

RHYTHMIC ANALYSIS—continued

TABLE 21.—TIME UNIT OF DRUM OR MORACHE [1]

Metronome—	Bear dance songs	Sun dance and undetermined dance songs	Social dance songs	Songs used in treatment of sick	War songs	Hand game songs	Parade and miscellaneous songs	Ute songs		Chippewa and Sioux songs		Chippewa, Sioux, and Ute songs	
								Number	Per cent	Number	Per cent	Number	Per cent
56					1			1		2	1	2	1
58	1							1				1	2
60			1		1		1	5	2	4	1	5	1
63	2				2		1	4	2	4	1	9	2
66	1		1					1	3	5	1	9	2
69								1	2	1		2	2
72		2	2					2	2	6	2	8	2
76		1	3		1		3	3	3	10	3	13	3
80			1					4	5	22	6	26	6
84		1	2				1	5	6	10	3	15	3
88		1	1		1			5	8	22	6	27	6
92			1				2	3	8	28	8	31	7
96							1	2	5	31	8	33	8
100						1	1	2	3	20	5	22	5
104	2		4			1	2	9	14	35	10	44	10
108	1		1		1			3	5	30	8	33	8
112			2			1		3	5	27	7	30	7
116			1			1		2	3	27	7	29	7
120	1				2	1	1	3	5	24	7	27	6
126								3	5	14	4	17	4
132		1					1	2	3	17	5	19	4

	Bear dance songs	Sun dance and undetermined dance songs	Social dance songs	Songs used in treatment of sick	War songs	Hand game songs	Parade and miscellaneous songs	Ute songs Number	Ute songs Per cent	Chippewa and Sioux songs Number	Chippewa and Sioux songs Per cent	Chippewa, Sioux, and Ute songs Number	Chippewa, Sioux, and Ute songs Per cent
138										8	2	8	2
144								1	2	5	1	6	1
152								1	2	4	1	5	1
160										4	1	4	1
168										5	1	5	1
176:										1		1	
Drum or morache not recorded²	7	6	2	15	7	3	5	45		234		279	
Total	17	12	22	15	16	9	19	110		600		710	

¹ In songs Nos. 72, 86, 87, and 88 the indicated tempo was preceded by a few measures on tremolo drumbeat. (See No. 72.)
² Excluded in computing percentage.

TABLE 22.—COMPARISON OF TIME UNIT OF VOICE AND DRUM

	Bear dance songs	Sun dance and undetermined dance songs	Social dance songs	Songs used in treatment of sick	War songs	Hand game songs	Parade and miscellaneous songs	Ute songs Number	Ute songs Per cent	Chippewa and Sioux songs Number	Chippewa and Sioux songs Per cent	Chippewa, Sioux, and Ute songs Number	Chippewa, Sioux, and Ute songs Per cent
Metronome—													
Time unit of voice and drum the same	9	6	18		7	5	13	58	89	163	45	221	51
Voice faster than drum	1	1			1			5	8	65	18	70	8
Voice slower than drum			2		1	1	1	2	3	138	38	140	32
Drum not recorded¹	7	6	2	15	7	3	5	45		234		279	
Total	17	12	22	15	16	9	19	110		600		710	

¹ Excluded in computing percentage.

COMPARISON OF ANALYSES OF UTE SONGS WITH ANALYSES OF CHIPPEWA AND SIOUX SONGS

TABLE 1.—Since the Ute songs are those of a tribe less advanced in civilization than the Chippewa and Sioux, it is interesting to note that they show a much higher percentage in major tonality. Reference to Tables 11 and 12 will show the proportion of major thirds to be also larger in the Ute songs than in those of the other tribes under analysis.

TABLES 2 AND 3.—These tables combine to show what may be termed the boundaries of the melody. In the Ute songs the initial tones of the songs, in about 75 per cent, are either the keynote, its third, fifth, or octave, and 50 per cent end on the keynote. In the Chippewa and Sioux songs the preference is for the twelfth and fifth, with the octave and tenth next in frequency. It will readily be seen that the Chippewa and Sioux songs are of wider range, what would be called in musical terminology the *tonic chord* being given in the upper octave. In Bulletin 61, page 42, attention was directed to the fact that the octave, twelfth, second octave, and its major third are the first, second, third, and fourth upper partial tones, or *overtones*, of a fundamental. The relatively large proportion of Chippewa and Sioux songs beginning on the twelfth suggested a feeling for the second overtone, the fifth representing the same scale-degree in the lower octave and occurring in songs having a compass of less than 12 tones. The compass of Ute songs is smaller than that of the songs previously analyzed. (See Table 5.) The reason for this must remain a matter of speculation. The environment of the Ute is entirely different from that of the other tribes under consideration, which adds interest to the radical differences appearing in some of the characteristics of the songs.

TABLE 4.—The lower percentage of Ute songs in which the final tone is the lowest tone counterbalances to some degree the higher percentage of Chippewa and Sioux songs ending on the keynote, as shown in Table 3. In the Ute songs the tone lower than the final tone does not immediately precede it in a majority of instances but occurs during the progress of the melody.

TABLE 5.—A high percentage of Ute songs have a compass of six, eight, and nine tones. It will be noted that only 30 per cent of the Ute songs have a compass of more than nine tones, while 57 per cent of the Chippewa and Sioux songs have such a compass.

TABLE 6.—It is interesting to observe that although the Ute songs have a higher percentage in major tonality they have a lower percentage of songs on the fourth five-toned ("major pentatonic") scale. Instead of finding the major songs in the pentatonic group, we find them in the succeeding groups which comprise songs with only four tones, these being the major triad and one additional tone. Comparison shows the Chippewa and Sioux songs to be much below the Ute in the percentage of these major four-toned songs. The five-toned scales mentioned in these analyses are the five pentatonic scales designated and named by Helmholtz. These five scales contain the same tones, but differ in keynote. (See Bull. 61, p. 7.)

TABLE 7.—Only 4 per cent of the Ute songs contain tones chromatically altered ("accidentals"), and the only tones thus altered are the fourth and seventh, which are raised a semitone. Among the Chippewa and Sioux songs the most frequent accidental is the sixth lowered a semitone, next in frequency being the fourth and seventh raised a semitone. The lowering of the submediant suggests a clearer musical perception than the raising of the fourth and seventh, as it suggests a change from major to minor tonality, further suggested by the lowering of the third in 6 per cent of the songs. The raising of the seventh makes it a "leading tone," but does not affect the tonality of the song. The singing of the fourth above the indicated pitch may have been due simply to an imperfect rendering of the interval.

TABLE 8.—The percentage of songs of a mixed form is more than twice as great in the Ute as in the Chippewa and Sioux. A better comparison lies in the percentage of melodic, which is much smaller, and harmonic, which is slightly larger, in the Ute.

TABLES 9 AND 10.—The proportion of songs beginning with an upward or downward progression is identical in the Ute and the tribes previously analyzed, and the difference in proportion of upward and downward intervals is too small to be of significance.

TABLES 11 AND 12.—In Table 11 (downward progressions) it is important to note that the proportion of major seconds is practically the same in the Ute as in the songs formerly analyzed. The Ute do not use intervals larger than a major sixth, which appear with some degree of frequency in the songs of the other tribes under consideration, but they do not substitute a large percentage of whole tones and semitones. Instead we find in the Ute songs an increased proportion of fifths, fourths, and major thirds, the minor thirds being smaller in percentage than in the other tribes. If small intervals preceded larger intervals in the formation of primitive music, we should expect to find a preponderance of small intervals in the songs of a tribe which, like the Utes, is acknowledged to be still primitive in thought. The comparisons noted in the downward progressions are found with little variation in Table 12, which shows the percentages of intervals in upward progression. In both tables the minor third is the most frequent interval except the major second, which is usually a passing tone.

TABLE 13.—Although the tables next preceding have shown that the Ute do not use certain large intervals which are used by the other tribes under consideration, the average interval in the two groups or songs is almost the same, since both are slightly larger than a minof third (three semitones). This adds interest to the investigation of the minor third in Indian music. The minor (non-major) third has frequently been noted by explorers, as well as by students of primitive music.

TABLE 14.—The consideration of Indian music as being literally in a "key" is foreign to the present work; thus the term "tonality" is substituted for "key" in the first table of analysis. The songs are grouped in the present table chiefly to determine the pitch of the songs and to observe this pitch with relation to the compass of the voice. The term "key" is here used in its broad sense, as applicable to nonharmonic music, inclusive of modes. E major, E flat major, and G major show the highest percentages in Ute songs, the latter being also the highest percentage in the Chippewa and Sioux songs.

TABLES 15 AND 16.—The Ute songs show a much higher proportion beginning on the accented portion of the measure—a peculiarity which suggests simplicity and directness. This is further shown by the higher percentage of songs beginning in 2–4 time, this being 62 per cent in the Ute and 54 per cent in the Chippewa and Sioux songs.

TABLE 17.—Only 11 per cent of the Ute songs contain no change of measure-lengths; 16 per cent of the songs previously analyzed are continuous in time. The difference between these proportions is of less interest than the fact that a change of measure-lengths appears to be so general a custom in all the tribes under analysis.

TABLE 18.—The accompanying instrument among the Utes seems to be primarily for the purpose of marking the time and to have less individuality than the accompanying instruments of the tribes previously analyzed. Thus the percentage of quarter-note drum rhythm in the Ute songs is more than three times that in the former group. The proportion of the eighth-note rhythm is somewhat smaller in the Ute, which shows less than one-third the percentage of songs in which the accompanying instrument is in a triplet count-division.

TABLE 19.—This is one of the most important tables of analysis, showing the rhythmic structure of the song, as Table 8 shows its melodic structure. In this table we note that in the recorded Ute songs the percentage containing a rhythmic unit is higher than in the Chippewa and Sioux. The melodic material of the Ute is shown to be less varied, the melodic structure less free, the drum rhythm simpler. In this connection it is interesting to note that the sense of rhythm is more prominent in the Ute songs. Two rhythmic units seem preferred to one, as the percentage of songs with one rhythmic unit is slightly less, while the proportion of songs with two rhythmic units is three times as great in the Ute as in the former groups.

TABLES 20 AND 21.—From these tables it appears that a tempo of 104 beats per minute is preferred by the Utes in their songs and also in the accompanying instrument.

TABLE 22.—A much greater similarity of tempo between voice and accompanying instrument appears in the Ute than in the Chippewa and Sioux songs, the percentage of songs in which both have the same tempo being 89 in the Ute and only 45 in the former songs. When voice and drum differ the drum is slower than the voice among the Utes and in large proportion is faster than the voice among the other tribes under consideration.

Summary of analysis.—From the foregoing it appears that, in comparison with Chippewa and Sioux songs, the Ute songs are more frequently major in tonality, harmonic in structure, and characterized by one or more rhythmic units. The compass is smaller and the intervals less varied, but the proportion of ascending and descending intervals is about the same. The average interval is smaller, but the difference is too slight to be of importance. The rhythm of the accompanying instrument is less varied, and its beat is more frequently synchronous with the voice.

Among the characteristics of the Ute songs which do not appear in the tables of analysis may be noted the connective phrase (p. 64), the downward glissando tone (p. 58), the upward glissando tone (p. 175), the interrupted drumbeat at certain points in the song (p. 97), and the peculiar monotonous rhythm described in the analysis of No. 2. The songs used in the treatment of the sick contain, as an entire group, certain interesting peculiarities which are noted in the section on that subject.

COMPARISON OF ANALYSES OF CHIPPEWA, SIOUX, AND UTE SONGS WITH ANALYSES OF SLOVAK SONGS

In order that the structure of Indian songs might be compared with that of European folk songs, the writer obtained a group of Slovak songs and analyzed them according to the method used in analyzing Indian songs. Dr. Aleš Hrdlička recommended the use of Slovak songs for this test, as the Slovak is one of the most isolated and racially pure groups of the Slavs, living in the foothills of the Carpathians. There they pursued their own manner of life from the dawn of history until disturbed to some degree by Magyarization, which began about a century ago. The songs used in the test were selected for the purpose by Mr. Ivan Daxner, secretary of the Slovenian League of America. They comprise a group of 10 songs, including the Slovak national anthem; a song concerning Janošik, the people's hero; a very ancient melody, "In praise of song"; a "dialogue on melody"; several love songs; and folk songs concerning the plowboy and the girl who watched the geese.

On comparing the structural analyses of tne Slovak and Indian songs we find the resemblances to be less than the differences, suggesting a widely different temperament in the peoples of the two races. These differences are much greater than between the songs of the several Indian tribes analyzed by the writer.

Considering first the resemblances, we find that the percentage of songs with a compass of an octave is 30 in the Slovak and varies from 21 to 35 in the Indian, except in a small group of Sioux songs recorded by Chippewa, in which it is smaller. There is also a resemblance in the proportions of ascending and descending major thirds and major seconds and in the ascending fourths. Among the differences we note that the minor third, which is so prominent in the Indian songs, occurs from one-fourth to one-half as frequently in the Slovak songs, while the minor second occurs from three to four times as frequently. The average interval in the Slovak songs is smaller than in the songs of any Indian tribe under analysis. In this connection it is interesting to note the contrast in the environment of the Slovaks and the Indians, the former, whose analyzed songs are characterized by a one-semitone interval, being a sedentary and agricultural people, and the latter, whose analyzed songs are characterized by a three-semitone interval (see p. 42), being a nomadic people, whose principal industries were hunting and fishing. The musical instinct is strongly marked in both peoples, and is part of the heritage of all the Slavs.

The proportion of descending intervals and the proportion of songs beginning with a descending progression is much smaller in the Slovak than in the Indian songs, suggesting that the descending trend, characteristic of Indian songs, is not characteristic of Slovak songs. The change of measure lengths, occurring in 85 per cent of the Indian songs, is entirely absent from the Slovak. The percentage of songs beginning on the accented portion of the measure and of those beginning in 2–4 time is much greater in the Slovak than in the Indian songs.

From the foregoing it appears that the Indian and Slovak songs under analysis differ in trend and in the principal interval of progression. It also appears that the Slovak songs have more directness in beginning and more simplicity of rhythm.

THE BEAR DANCE

The characteristic dance of the Ute Indians is the Bear dance, which is held every year in the early spring. The intention is to hold the dance at about the time that the bear comes from his hibernation,

a, Entrance to Bear dance inclosure

b, Last portion of Bear dance

c, Last portion of Bear dance

a, Sun dance pole

b, Sun dance pole with portion of brush shelter

SUN DANCE GROUND

yet the Indians seem to expect that snow will fall either during or soon after the dance. Some informants stated that the Bear dance was formerly in the nature of a courting dance, but sociability and general good feeling appear to be its chief characteristics at the present time. The custom of the Northern Utes seems to differ little from that of the Southern Utes as described by Verner Z. Reed,[15] who witnessed the Bear dance on their reservation in Colorado in March, 1893.

The Bear dance is held in a large circular space inclosed by a barrier formed of upright poles, between which the branches of trees are woven horizontally. The inclosure used for the Bear dance in 1914 was visited by the writer. (Pl. 8, a.) The walls were about 9 feet in height and the inclosure about 200 feet in diameter. At the side opposite the door was an excavation in the ground about 5 feet long, 2 feet wide, and 2 feet deep. Over this, during the dance, there had been placed sheets of zinc on which the singers, seated around the sides, rested their morache. (See pl. 1.) This hollow (or cave) in the ground was said to be "connected with the bear," and the rasping sound produced by the morache was said to be "like the sound made by a bear."

During the week which precedes a Bear dance the people rehearse the dancing. When the dance is formally opened they don all their finery and continue dancing for several days. The dancers take their places in parallel lines facing each other, the men in one line and the women in the other. They do not touch each other, neither do they progress during the dancing until the last day of the dance. If a dancer falls from exhaustion or from a misstep, the singing ceases and a medicine man or the leader of the dancers "restores the dancer." Taking a morache from one of the singers, he places the lower end of the notched stick against the body of the prostrate man and passes the rubbing stick rapidly up and down upon it. He begins this at the dancer's feet and repeats the motion upward until the man's head is reached, when he holds the notched stick toward the sky and passes the rubbing stick upward as though he were brushing something from the notched stick into the air. Sometimes two or more of these treatments are necessary before the man rises and resumes dancing. He is not required to give a present to the man who thus "restores" him.

On the final day of the dance, soon after sunrise, a man and a woman chase each other around the inclosure, and if they see anyone laugh at them it is the custom for them to appear ferocious, running toward the person and pretending to scratch him. Sometimes they apply red paint around the mouth to look as though blood were dripping from the jaws, suggesting the ferocity of the bear. The

---

[15] Reed, Verner Z., The Ute Bear Dance. Amer. Anthropologist, vol. 9, 1896.

manner of dancing changes on this day, the line of women approaching the line of men and attempting to push them backward. Then each woman tries to push the man who stands opposite her. (Pl. 8, *b*, *c*.) After a time the women succeed in pushing the men across their side of the inclosure and against the wall. This marks the conclusion of the dance.

CHARACTERISTICS OF SONGS

The chief characteristic of these songs is a glissando on downward progressions which was said to "imitate the sound made by a bear." This glissando appears most frequently on the descending interval of a fourth, an interval which, in Chippewa songs, was found to be prominent in songs concerning animals.[16] The intervals of progression are small, 78 per cent being a major third or intervals smaller than a major third. All the songs contain a rhythmic unit. showing the rhythmic sense to be stronger than the melodic. Several of the songs contain a "singsong" type of rhythm in the latter portion, if not in the entire song. This monotonous rhythm is a contrast to the intelligent, thematic treatment of rhythm noted in many Chippewa and Sioux songs.

No. 1. " The Dust of the Red Wagon "   (Catalogue No. 758)

Recorded by SINGER No. 1

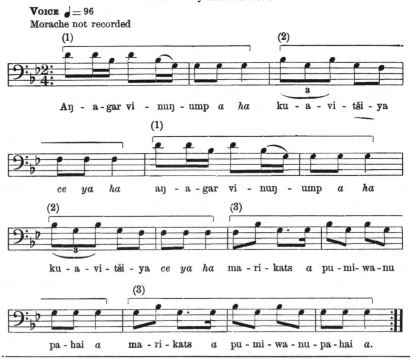

VOICE ♩ = 96
Morache not recorded

Aŋ - a - gar vi - nuŋ - ump a ha ku - a - vi - tši - ya

ce ya ha aŋ - a - gar vi - nuŋ - ump a ha

ku - a - vi - tši - ya ce ya ha ma - ri - kats a pu - mi - wa - nu

pa - hai a ma - ri - kats a pu - mi - wa - nu - pa - hai a.

---

[16] See Bull. 53, p. 101.

WORDS

a′ŋagar......................red
vi′nuŋump....................wagon
ku′avi′tšiya..................dust
ma′rikatš....................white man
pumi′wanupahai.............looking around

Analysis.—This melody comprises six rhythmic periods, the first four containing two measures each and the last two containing three measures each. The final measure in every period contains two eighth notes followed by a quarter note. This phrase is sung on the lowest tone in the period which, with its frequent recurrence, gives the phrase a certain emphasis. Noting the tones on which this occurs we find them to be G, F, G, F, G, G. The tones in the first, third, fifth, and sixth periods are those of the triad of G minor, and the song is analyzed in that key. The melody progresses chiefly by thirds, 63 per cent of the intervals being minor and 22 per cent major thirds.

No. 2. Yellow Hair   (Catalogue No. 784)

Recorded by SINGER No. 2

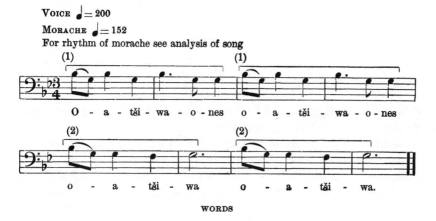

WORDS

oa′tšiwa′ones..................yellow hair sticking up

The words of this song may refer to the appearance of a bear.

Analysis.—This song is characterized by a monotonous rhythm and a lack of variety in melodic progression. Other songs containing the same characteristics are Nos. 3, 4, 6, 10, 15, and 16 in the Bear dance songs, and a majority of the hand game songs, Nos. 94–102. This rhythmic and melodic peculiarity suggests a vocal expression scarcely developed to the point of composed song. We find in it a resemblance to the rhythmic vocalization which accompanies concerted labor among peoples low in the scale of culture. In a majority of the songs cited the principal interval is the minor (or nonmajor) third, which characterizes the most primitive vocal expression of uncivilized peoples. (See Bull. 53, p. 7.) This interval is prominent also in the early music of civilization. The tone material of this song comprises a fundamental (G), with its minor third and minor seventh—a tone material not previously noted by the writer. For convenience the song is analyzed as in the key of G minor, though it can scarcely be said to constitute a key in the accepted sense of that term.

The rhythm of the notched-stick rattle is simple and does not vary in the songs recorded with its accompaniment. The rubbing stick is thrust downward upon the notched stick, producing a sharp, rasping sound, and as it is brought upward, preparatory to the next stroke, there is a similar but less pronounced sound, the downward stroke occupying a period of time slightly longer than that required for returning the rubbing stick to its original position. The sound produced by the upward motion varied with individuals, those who used he rattle with special energy producing, of course, a louder sound with the upward motion of the rubbing stick. The song under analysis is the only recorded Bear dance song in which the rattle and voice are not synchronous at the beginning of each count. In this song the tempo of the rattle is slightly slower than that of the voice.

This and the song next following are examples of recent composition among the Utes. Fred Mart, the writer's interpreter, said that he composed these songs "in dreams." This manner of composing songs was customary in the old days and has been noted among many tribes of Indians. The usage among Chippewa and Sioux is noted in Bulletin 53, page 37, and Bulletin 61, page 59. It is not uncommon among the Utes at the present time.

Concerning the origin of this song, Mr. Mart said: "I dreamed that I was at a Bear dance; there was a great crowd, but they were strangers to me and did not address me. All were singing this song and I learned it from them. I sang it while I was still asleep and was singing it aloud when I awoke. After that I remembered the song." In explanation of the words, he said: "Many Utes wear a flat, polished shell suspended around their necks, and at the Bear dance they tie a weasel skin to this shell. The idea of the word is, 'Dance harder so your weasel skin will swing faster.'" Mr. Mart taught this song to the singers at a Bear dance, and when it was sung the old people mistook it for an old song. It was necessary for him to sing it only two or three times with the singers at the drum, after which he led them in the singing of it. When recording the song, he shouted between the renditions, "Dance harder, Red Stick," as though addressing a dancer, and "That is the way to dance," it being customary to urge the dancers in this manner.

No. 3. " Dance faster "   (Catalogue No. 772)

Recorded by SINGER No. 3

Voice ♩ = 104

MORACHE. ♩ = 104

Rhythm of morache similar to No. 2

Pa - vi - tsu   *a*   pa - vi - tsu   *a*   puŋ - ke   ya-mi - ko - va - ni

WORDS

pāvi′tšu......................weasel skin
puŋke........................hard (or fast)
yamiko′vani..................swing (imperative verb)

Analysis.—This song, in contrast to that next preceding, is characterized by the interval of the major third, which constitutes 52 per cent of the intervals. Next in frequency is the interval of a fourth, constituting 27 per cent of the entire number. The rhythmic unit is short and occurs in both double and triple measures. Countdivisions similar to those in the rhythmic unit appear throughout the song. The melody tones are those of the major triad and fourth. The low G at the close of the song was given with distinctness, though it seemed to be below the natural compass of the singer's voice. No variation occurred in the four renditions of this melody. The interval of a fourth characterizes this song and is also prominent in Nos. 7, 11, 16, 20, 50, 88, 90, and 100. A monotonous rhythm somewhat resembling that of the present song is noted also in Nos. 4, 6, 10, 15, 16, 42, 98, and 101. This peculiarity was not found in songs of the Chippewa and Sioux.

Concerning the origin of the following song, Mr. Mart said: "I dreamed I was visiting far away. A woman was with me and we were at a great dance of all the tribes, each led by a chief. Our tribe was led by Nu'šina. He was then a spirit, but when he was alive he was a medicine man. In my dream we were dancing in a great circle and Nu'šina sang this song, and we sang it with him until I learned it. I was singing aloud when I awoke from my dream." The words of the song are simple but suggest a connection with a medicine man.

No. 4. Song of Nu'šina   (Catalogue No. 773)

Recorded by SINGER No. 3

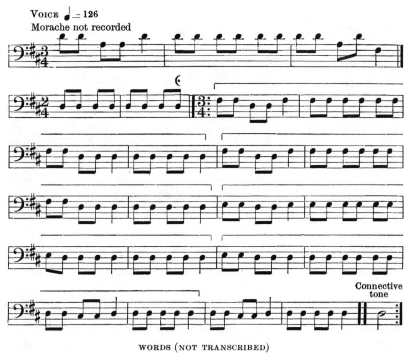

WORDS (NOT TRANSCRIBED)

kwa'nantš.....................eagle
pututš.......................down

Analysis.—Two renditions of this song were recorded and are uniform in every respect. This is interesting, as the rhythmic unit is long and the measure-divisions monotonous. In numerous Ute songs there occurs a connective phrase, sung between renditions of the melody. In some instances a connective tone is sung midway of the ascent from the final tone of the song to that with which the repetition begins. In this instance the connective tone is on the same pitch as the lowest tone of the melody. A wide variety of intervals occurs in the song, a peculiarity which was noted in the more modern Sioux songs.　Thus we find five sorts of ascending and four of descending intervals, while in the song next preceding, which was mistaken for an old song, almost 80 per cent of the intervals were fourths and major thirds.　This song is melodic in structure and contains the tones of the fourth five-toned scale.

No. 5. Bear Dance Song (a)　　　(Catalogue No. 690)

Recorded by SINGER No. 4

Analysis.—The somewhat monotonous rhythm of this song is varied only by a triple measure near the close.　The melody tones are those of the fourth five-toned scale, and the ascending and descending intervals are about equal in number.　Major and minor thirds constitute 89 per cent of the intervals, though the fourth is prominent in a portion of the melody.　Five renditions were recorded and show no variations.

No. 6. Bear Dance Song (b)　　　(Catalogue No. 691)

Recorded by SINGER No. 4

Analysis.—This song is harmonic in structure, containing only the tones of the major triad and the fourth, which is always raised a semitone. The rapid phrases in which this tone occurs were given without variation in the four renditions of the song. In tonality the song is major, and 57 per cent of the intervals are major thirds. The rhythmic form of the song is interesting and clear, with four occurrences of the rhythmic unit.

No. 7. Bear Dance Song (c)   (Catalogue No. 692)

Recorded by SINGER No. 4

VOICE ♩ = 104
Morache not recorded

Connective phrase

Analysis.—In the renditions of this melody we have an example of the "connective phrase" found in Ute music and not in that of the Chippewa and Sioux previously analyzed by the writer. Similar phrases are transcribed in songs Nos. 39 (duplication), 41, 46, 70, 72, 84, 85, 86, 89, 91, 92, and 93. A connective tone has been mentioned in the analysis of No. 4. This connective phrase was sung slightly rubato in its two final measures and occurs between all the six renditions of the song. It can not be considered an introductory phrase, as the singer began with the first measure of the melody as transcribed. Among the Chippewa and Sioux it was not unusual to find an introductory phrase, which was sung before the first rendition of the song and omitted in all the subsequent renditions.

The rhythm of this song is clear and forceful, the two units being distinctly given. Thirty-eight progressions occur in the song, all but two of which are fourths and major thirds. (See No. 3.) The melody tones are those of the major triad and second.

No. 8. Bear Dance Song (d)   (Catalogue No. 763)

Recorded by SINGER No. 5

VOICE ♩ = 104

MORACHE ♩ = 104
Rhythm of morache similar to No. 2

Analysis.—A peculiarity of this song is the rest during which, in the four renditions of the song, the voice was silent while the scraping of the rattle continued in exact time. Two rhythmic units occur, and count-divisions similar to those of the units appear throughout the melody. About half the progressions are whole and half tones, which is unusual. The melody contains all the tones of the octave except the sixth and seventh. The descending intervals of a fourth were sung glissando in this as in numerous other songs of the Bear dance. This glissando was said to "imitate the sound made by a bear." Other songs containing rests are Nos. 11, 19, 27, 41, 46, 48, 68, 77, 94, 95, 96, and 97.

25043°—22——5

No. 9. Bear Dance Song (e)   (Catalogue No. 764)

Recorded by SINGER No. 5

VOICE ♩ = 108

MORACHE ♩ = 108

Rhythm of morache similar to No. 2

The Ute words of this song were said to mean "As the sun comes up it raises a dust." These words were not recorded.

Analysis.—The tone material of this song comprises a fundamental with its minor third, fourth, and minor seventh. Progression is chiefly by thirds, which constitute 86 per cent of the intervals. The song contains four rhythmic periods and four closing measures. This form is accurately repeated in the three renditions of the song. Rattle and voice have the same tempo and were synchronous on the first of each count.

No. 10. Bear Dance Song (f) (Catalogue No. 765)

Recorded by SINGER No. 5

VOICE ♩ = 58
MORACHE ♩ = 58
Rhythm of morache similar to No. 2

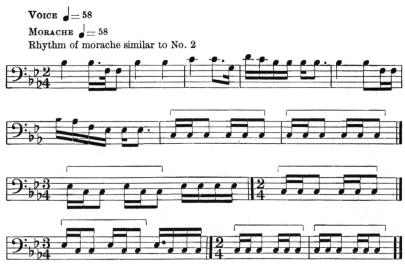

Analysis.—All the tones of the octave occur in this song, which is minor in tonality and melodic in structure. The opening tone is the seventh, followed by a descending fourth sung glissando. This is an unusual opening but is uniform in the four renditions of the song. About 65 per cent of the progressions are thirds, though the fourth is prominent in the first part of the song. The rhythmic unit is short and in itself uninteresting, but the triple measures give variety and character to the rhythm of the song as a whole. The tempo of the song is unusually slow.

No. 11. Bear Dance Song (g)   (Catalogue No. 766)

Recorded by SINGER No. 5

Analysis.—Four renditions of this song were recorded and in them all occur the changes of tempo indicated in the transcription. The first of the slower phrases is on a tone which appears to have little relation to the rest of the melody, but this tone was persistent in the several renditions. Two rhythmic units occur, having the same division of the first count but differing in the remaining portion. The fourth is a prominent interval, comprising 25 per cent of the entire number. (See No. 3.) Attention is directed to the ascent of a ninth, midway through the song. Reference to Table 12 on page 41 will show this to be an unusual progression. The song is melodic in structure and contains the tones of the second five-toned scale. Other songs containing rests are noted in the analysis of No. 8. Other songs containing a change of tempo are Nos. 76 and 99.

No. 12. Bear Dance Song (h)   (Catalogue No. 739)

Recorded by SINGER No. 6

VOICE ♩ = 66
MORACHE ♩ = 66
Rhythm of morache similar to No. 2

Analysis.—The rhythmic unit of this song occurs only twice, the second time being on a pitch slightly lower than the first. Count-divisions similar to those of the unit occur throughout the song. Seven renditions were recorded with no variation except that the sixteenth note followed by an eighth note was not always clear in relative time value. The fourth is prominent in the structure of the melody, though almost half the progressions are whole tones. The song has a compass of nine tones and contains all the tones of the octave except the seventh.

No. 13. Bear Dance Song (i)   (Catalogue N o. 740

Recorded by SINGER No. 6

VOICE ♩ = 63
MORACHE ♩ = 63
Rhythm of morache similar to No. 2

Analysis.—This is a pleasing melody containing the tones of the fourth five-toned scale. Six renditions were recorded, the time being continuous throughout the performance. The wide variety of intervals suggests that the song may be modern, since that peculiarity characterized Sioux songs which were known to be less than 50 years old. This song contains five sorts of ascending and five of descending intervals. The glissando manner of singing was especially marked in this instance.

No. 14. Bear Dance Song (j)   (Catalogue No. 730)

Recorded by SINGER No. 7

VOICE ♩ = 63 (♪ = 126)

MORACHE ♩ = 63

Rhythm of morache similar to No. 2

Analysis.—Although 87 per cent of the progressions in this song are minor thirds and major seconds, the melody is varied and interesting, with a compass of nine tones. The rhythmic unit comprises an entire octave. Three renditions were recorded, in all of which the measure transcribed in 5–8 time was sung as indicated. Only one other song (No. 27) contains 5–8 measures.

No. 15. Bear Dance Song (k)   (Catalogue No. 773)

Recorded by SINGER No. 8

VOICE ♩ = 120

MORACHE ♩ = 120

Rhythm of morache similar to No. 2

(1)   (1)   (2)

(2)

Analysis.—In rhythm this song is typical of the monotonous type of Bear dance song which could be continued indefinitely. (See No. 2.) The two rhythmic units are alike except that in the second there is a concluding measure which gives balance to the rhythm of the song as a whole. With one exception the progressions are major and minor thirds. Several renditions were recorded and show no points of difference.

No. 16. Final Song of Bear Dance (a)   (Catalogue No. 774)

Recorded by SINGER No. 3

VOICE ♩ = 72
Morache not recorded

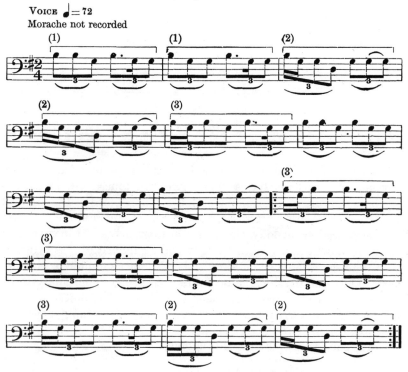

Analysis.—The rhythm of this song is unusually interesting. It will be noted that the first and third rhythmic units have the same division of the second count and that the second and third units have the same division of the first count. The even triplet division of certain measures can not be considered a unit of rhythm, as a triplet occurs in the first measure of the first unit. This rhythmic structure does not vary in the several renditions of the song. Sixty-five progressions occur, the only intervals being the fourth and the major third. (See Nos. 3 and 17.) The song has a compass of six tones and contains only the tones of the major triad.

No. 17. Final Song of Bear Dance (b)   (Catalogue No. 693)

Recorded by SINGER NO. 4

VOICE $\quad \downarrow = 144$

MORACHE $\quad \downarrow = 144$

Rhythm of morache similar to No. 2

Analysis.—This, like the song next preceding, is major in tonality, harmonic in structure, has a compass of six tones, and progresses only by intervals of the fourth and the major third. The present melody contains 15 progressions, 53 per cent of which are downward, and the preceding melody contains 67 progressions, 51 per cent of which are downward. With these melodic similarities it is interesting to note the difference between the rhythmic character of the two songs. Only one rhythmic unit occurs in the song under analysis, its four repetitions comprising the entire melody. The preceding song contains three short rhythmic units with many intervening measures. The present song contains eight changes of measure lengths, while the preceding song is in 2–4 time throughout.

PLOTS OF BEAR DANCE SONGS [17]

In the plots of a large majority of the Bear dance songs we note a resemblance to the plots of Sioux songs concerning animals. (See Bull. 61, p. 204.) This resemblance consists in the touching of a low

---

[17] A form of graphic representation, or "plotting," of melodies has been devised by the writer for the purpose of making the trend of melodies more apparent. The general method employed is similar to that used in showing graphically the course of a moving object. The loci of the object at given periods of time are determined and recorded, the several positions being connected by straight lines. In any use of this method the interest centers in the several points at which the object is located, it being understood that the lines connecting these points are used merely as an aid to observation. In the present adaptation of this method the pitch of the accented tones in a melody is indicated by dots placed at the intersection of coordinate lines, the horizontal coordinates representing scale degrees and the vertical coordinates representing measure lengths. These dots are connected by straight lines, though the progress of the melody between the accented tones would, in many instances, vary widely from these lines if it were accurately plotted. The use of accented tones exclusively in analyzing these songs has already been employed, the structure of the melodies being determined by the pitch of contiguous accented tones. One of the reasons which seem to justify this usage is the observation that, when differences appear in the several renditions of an Indian song, these differences usually are found to be in unimportant progressions between unaccented tones. Since the sole purpose of these plots is to show the trend of the melodies, it seems permissible to omit from the representation, not only the unaccented tones occurring in the melody, but also a distinction between whole tones and semitones in progressions, and a distinction between double and triple time in measure lengths. It is obviously desirable that the graphic representation be as simple as possible, the more detailed observation of the melodies being contained in the tabulated and descriptive analyses.

point and immediately rising to a higher one. This, in the outline, may suggest the bounding or leaping of an animal. In the Bear dance songs, however, the higher point of such a series is more uniform than

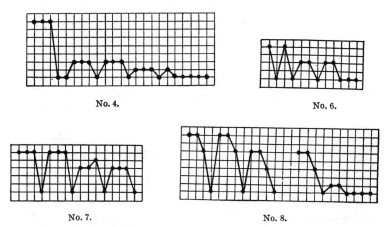

No. 4.   No. 6.

No. 7.   No. 8.

FIG. 1.—Plots, Group 1 (Bear dance)

in the Sioux songs, producing what might be termed a "horizontal type" of plot. This appears in a less marked degree in the plots of the hand game song. (See p. 181.)

TABULATED ANALYSIS OF BEAR DANCE SONGS

MELODIC ANALYSIS

TABLE 1A.—TONALITY

	Number of songs	Serial Nos. of songs
Major tonality	12	3, 4, 5, 6, 7, 8, 12, 13, 14, 15, 16, 17.
Minor tonality	5	1, 2, 9, 10, 11.
Total	17	

TABLE 2A.—FIRST NOTE OF SONG—ITS RELATION TO KEYNOTE

	Number of songs	Serial Nos. of songs
Beginning on the—		
Octave	2	3, 4.
Seventh	1	10.
Sixth	1	14.
Fifth	3	1, 6, 11.
Third	8	2, 7, 8, 12, 13, 15, 16, 17.
Second	1	5.
Keynote	1	9.
Total	17	

TABULATED ANALYSIS OF BEAR DANCE SONGS—Continued

MELODIC ANALYSIS—continued

TABLE 3A.—LAST NOTE OF SONG—ITS RELATION TO KEYNOTE

	Number of songs	Serial Nos. of songs
Ending on the—		
Fifth	6	7, 8, 12, 13, 14, 15.
Third	1	9.
Keynote	10	1, 2, 3, 4, 5, 6, 10, 11, 16, 17.
Total	17	

TABLE 4A.—LAST NOTE OF SONG—ITS RELATION TO COMPASS OF SONG

	Number of songs	Serial Nos. of songs
Songs in which final tone is—		
Lowest tone in song	7	5, 6, 7, 8, 10, 14, 16.
Immediately preceded by—		
Fourth below	3	3, 11, 17.
Minor third below	1	15.
Whole tone below	1	2.
Semitone below	1	4.
Whole tone below with fourth below in previous measure	1	12.
Whole tone below with minor third below in previous measure	1	13.
Songs containing a minor third below the final tone	1	9.
Songs containing a whole tone below the final tone	1	1.
Total	17	

TABLE 5A.—NUMBER OF TONES COMPRISING COMPASS OF SONG

	Number of songs	Serial Nos. of songs
Compass of—		
Eleven tones	1	3.
Nine tones	4	4, 10, 12, 14.
Eight tones	6	5, 8, 9, 11, 13, 15.
Six tones	4	1, 7, 16, 17.
Five tones	1	6.
Four tones	1	2.
Total	17	

TABULATED ANALYSIS OF BEAR DANCE SONGS—Continued

MELODIC ANALYSIS—continued

TABLE 6A.—TONE MATERIAL

	Number of songs	Serial Nos. of songs
Second five-toned scale	1	11.
Fourth five-toned scale	3	4, 5, 13.
Major triad	2	16, 17.
Major triad and sixth	2	1, 14.
Major triad and fourth	2	3, 6.
Major triad and second	1	7.
Octave complete	1	10.
Octave complete except seventh	1	12.
Octave complete except seventh and sixth	1	8.
Octave complete except sixth and fourth	1	15.
Minor third and seventh	1	2.
Minor seventh, fourth, and third	1	9.
Total	17	

TABLE 7A.—ACCIDENTALS

	Number of songs	Serial Nos. of songs
Songs containing—		
No accidentals	16	1, 2, 3, 4, 5, 7, 8, 9, 10, 11, 12, 13, 14, 15, 16, 17.
Fourth raised a semitone	1	6.
Total	17	

TABLE 8A.—STRUCTURE

	Number of songs	Serial Nos. of songs
Melodic	8	4, 5, 9, 10, 11, 12, 14, 15.
Melodic with harmonic framework	5	1, 3, 7, 8, 13.
Harmonic	4	2, 6, 16, 17.
Total	17	

TABLE 9A.—FIRST PROGRESSION—DOWNWARD AND UPWARD

	Number of songs	Serial Nos. of songs
Downward	15	1, 2, 3, 4, 6, 7, 9, 10, 11, 12, 13, 14, 15, 16, 17.
Upward	2	5, 8.
Total	17	

TABULATED ANALYSIS OF BEAR DANCE SONGS—Continued

MELODIC ANALYSIS—continued

TABLE 10A.—TOTAL NUMBER OF PROGRESSIONS—DOWNWARD AND UPWARD

	Number of songs	Serial Nos. of songs
Downward	283	
Upward	209	
Total	492	

TABLE 11A.—INTERVALS IN DOWNWARD PROGRESSION

	Number of songs	Serial Nos. of songs
Interval of a—		
Minor sixth	3	
Fifth	5	
Fourth	46	
Major third	95	
Minor third	57	
Major second	69	
Minor second	8	
Total	283	

TABLE 12A.—INTERVALS IN UPWARD PROGRESSION

	Number of songs	Serial Nos. of songs
Interval of a—		
Ninth	1	
Octave	2	
Seventh	1	
Major sixth	1	
Minor sixth	4	
Fifth	10	
Fourth	36	
Major third	69	
Minor third	40	
Major second	39	
Minor second	6	
Total	209	

TABLE 13A.—AVERAGE NUMBER OF SEMITONES IN AN INTERVAL

Total number of intervals.. 492
Total number of semitones.. 1,805
Average number of semitones in an interval.. 3.6

Tabulated Analysis of Bear Dance Songs—Continued

MELODIC ANALYSIS—continued

TABLE 14A.—KEY

	Number of songs	Serial Nos. of songs
Key of—		
A major	2	7, 14.
B flat major	2	5, 8.
C major	1	3.
C minor	2	9, 10.
D flat major	2	12, 13.
D major	1	4.
E flat major	1	17.
G flat major	1	6.
G major	2	15, 16.
G minor	2	1, 2.
G sharp minor	1	11.
Total	17	

RHYTHMIC ANALYSIS

TABLE 15A.—PART OF MEASURE ON WHICH SONG BEGINS

	Number of songs	Serial Nos. of songs
Beginning on unaccented part of measure	5	5, 6, 8, 12, 13.
Beginning on accented part of measure	12	1, 2, 3, 4, 7, 9, 10, 11, 14, 15, 16, 17.
Total	17	

TABLE 16A.—RHYTHM (METER) OF FIRST MEASURE

	Number of songs	Serial Nos. of songs
First measure in—		
2–4 time	11	1, 3, 5, 6, 7, 8, 9, 10, 13, 14, 16.
3–4 time	6	2, 4, 11, 12, 15, 17
Total	17	

TABULATED ANALYSIS OF BEAR DANCE SONGS—Continued

RHYTHMIC ANALYSIS—continued

TABLE 17A.—CHANGE OF TIME, MEASURE-LENGTHS

	Number of songs	Serial Nos. of songs
Songs containing no change of time	4	1, 2, 15, 16.
Songs containing a change of time	13	3, 4, 5, 6, 7, 8, 9, 10, 11, 12, 13, 14, 17.
Total	17	

TABLE 18A.—RHYTHM (METER) OF MORACHE

	Number of songs	Serial Nos. of songs
Downward stroke of rubbing stick in quarter note value	10	2, 3, 8, 9, 10, 12, 13, 14, 15, 17.
Morache not recorded	7	1, 4, 5, 6, 7, 11, 16.
Total	17	

TABLE 19A.—RHYTHMIC UNIT OF SONG

	Number of songs	Serial Nos. of songs
Songs containing—		
One rhythmic unit	9	3, 4, 5, 6, 10, 12, 13, 14, 17.
Two rhythmic units	6	2, 7, 8, 9, 11, 15.
Three rhythmic units	2	1, 16.
Total	17	

TABLE 20A.—TIME UNIT OF VOICE

	Number of songs	Serial Nos. of songs
Metronome—		
58	1	10.
63	2	13, 14.
66	1	12.
72	1	16.
76	1	6.
96	1	1.
104	4	3, 5, 7, 8.
108	1	9.
120	1	15.
126	1	4.
144	2	11, 17.
200	1	2.
Total	17	

TABULATED ANALYSIS OF BEAR DANCE SONGS—Continued

RHYTHMIC ANALYSIS—continued

TABLE 21A.—TIME UNIT OF MORACHE

	Number of songs	Serial Nos. of songs
Metronome—		
58	1	10.
63	2	13, 14.
66	1	12.
104	2	3, 8.
108	1	9.
120	1	15.
144	1	17.
152	1	2.
Morache not recorded	7	1, 4, 5, 6, 7, 11, 16.
Total	17	

TABLE 22A.—COMPARISON OF TIME UNIT OF VOICE AND MORACHE

	Number of songs	Serial Nos. of songs
Time unit of voice and morache the same	9	3, 8, 9, 10, 12, 13, 14, 15, 17.
Voice faster than morache	1	2.
Morache not recorded	7	1, 4, 5, 6, 7, 11, 16.
Total	17	

THE SUN DANCE

The Sun dance of the Utes is said to have been received by them from the Arapaho about the year 1902. It is held each year at the full moon, usually in June. A Sun dance was held on the Uinta and Ouray Reservation in June, 1914, against the orders of the Government. Plate 9 shows the place where this dance was held; also the pole and part of the brush inclosure. This place is on a level part of the high plateau, affording an ample place for camping. It is the same ground where Sun dances had been held for many years, and numerous poles were still standing when the place was visited by the writer.

No element of suffering entered into this dance beyond the effects of fasting and of long-continued dancing. No lacerations seem to have been practiced by the Utes at any period. The dance. was held by them for the curing of the sick. Many accounts of remarkable cures were related. It was said that "participation in the Sun dance would cure anything," but the disease most frequently mentioned in connection with it is rheumatism, which is prevalent on the reservation. On being asked how the cure was effected, Pa'gitš, a Ute medicine man, replied without hesitation, "They get better because they don't eat and drink for a while."

There was said to be no ceremony connected with the cutting of the tree for the Sun dance pole, but it was not permissible for the pole to touch the ground. After felling the tree the bark was removed, together with all the branches except "a few green leaves at the top" and a short branch near the top, to which was fastened some willow brush. When the pole had been carried to the camp it was lifted carefully and placed upright in the hole dug for that purpose. Around the Sun dance pole a lodge or shelter was constructed by erecting a wall of brush about 4 feet in height and placing poles from this to the Sun dance pole in the center. This lodge opened toward the east and the drum was at the left of the entrance.

In preparation for the ceremony the dancers painted their bodies, this paint being renewed every morning during the period of dancing. The manner of decoration was decided by individual taste. The designs were simple, no "pictures" or "zigzag lines" being used. Pa'gitš said that his design was "a line across the nose." Each dancer carried an eagle-bone whistle, to which was attached a white eagle plume. There was no decoration on the whistle.

The ceremony lasted four days and nights, during which time the dancers abstained from food and water and remained in the lodge. Occasionally the dance was terminated at the end of the third day, but four days was said to be the proper length of time. It was said that a "sham battle" was held early in the morning of the day that the Sun dance began. This was sometimes followed by a Dragging-feet dance, but no social dances were permitted in the camp after the opening of the Sun dance. The old men sometimes built a sweat lodge and went into it before the ceremony, but this was not a common custom.

A "parade" was held before the beginning of the Sun dance. In this, as in other parades (see p. 166), the participants were on horseback, the men preceding the women and beating hand drums as they sang. One song of this parade was recorded (No. 26).

Pa'gitš (pl. 10, c) said that 10 or 12 was the usual number of dancers and that they entered the lodge in the early evening, when "only a rim of the sun was above the horizon." There was no acknowledged leader of the ceremony, but a prayer was made by one of the men after they entered the lodge. He was said to "pray to the sun." This man did not sit by the pole, but sat wherever he liked. The man who prayed at the time of entering the lodge did not make another prayer during the ceremony, but others made prayers from time to time. It was required that these be men who had dreamed dreams. The first night the men danced until daylight. No one man danced all the time; yet there was never a time when some one was not dancing. Some men were able to dance as long as four hours at a time. The women did not dance, but sat with the men at the drum. Sometimes an old man arose and sang his personal song received in a dream. A dancer who had received a song in a dream might request his friends to learn it and sing it while he was dancing. The dancers did not look at the sun, but at the willow brush on the pole. If a man became exhausted he was allowed to sleep for a time.

At the end of the last day of the dance many gifts were bestowed in the lodge. Dancers often gave presents to spectators and expected no return. Occasionally a dancer received a horse or some equally valuable gift from another dancer, in return for which he "prayed to the sun" for the health of the donor. On this day a medicine man frequently took some of the dust that had been under the feet of the dancers and put it on the head of a sick person, waving an eagle feather over him, this treatment being considered of especial efficacy.

Relating his personal experience, Pa′gitš said that he had taken part in the Sun dance six times. His reason for doing this was a belief that some one had "poisoned him with rattlesnake poison," producing rheumatism. On the third day of dancing he "felt better." The entire period of his dancing, however, was four days and nights. He stated that he did not experience discomfort from fasting, but that the lack of water was hard to endure.

Words were sometimes used in Sun dance songs, but do not appear in the songs herewith presented. No. 23 was sung on the last day of the dancing, and No. 26, as already stated, is a song of the parade. The other songs were sung at any time during the Sun dance.

CHARACTERISTICS OF SONGS

Seventy-five per cent of the Sun dance songs are minor in tonality, yet only one song is on the second five-toned (minor pentatonic) scale. The melodic material is generous, one-third of the songs containing the entire octave and others lacking only one or two tones of the complete octave. In structure all these songs are either melodic or harmonic with melodic framework. A majority of the songs contain one or more rhythmic units.

25043°—22——6

No. 18. Sun Dance Song (a)   (Catalogue No. 694)

Recorded by SINGER No. 4

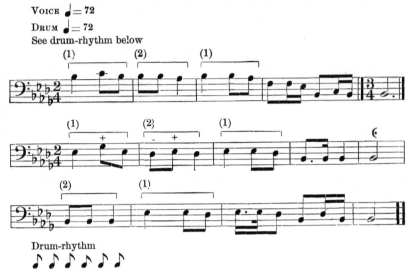

Voice ♩ = 72

Drum ♩ = 72

See drum-rhythm below

Drum-rhythm

Analysis.—Two rhythmic units occur in this song, the count-divisions of the first being reversed in the second. The song comprises three rhythmic periods, the first two containing five measures each and the third containing four measures. All the tones of the octave occur in the song, which is minor in tonality and progresses chiefly by whole tones. Voice and drum have the same tempo and are synchronous on the first of each count.

No. 19. Sun Dance Song (b)   (Catalogue No. 695)

Recorded by SINGER No. 4

Voice ♩ = 76

Drum ♩ = 76

Drum-rhythm similar to No. 18

Analysis.—The transcription of this song is from the fourth rendition. An interesting variation in previous renditions is that measures 5, 9, and 14 are frequently changed from double to triple measures by a repetition of the first count. The rest midway through the song was given distinctly in all the renditions. For other songs containing rests see No. 8. With three exceptions the progressions are thirds and major seconds, yet the melody has a range of 13 tones. The song is major in tonality and contains all the tones of the octave except the seventh.

No. 20. Sun Dance Song (c)   (Catalogue No. 700)

Recorded by SINGER No. 9

VOICE ♩ = 72
DRUM ♩ = 72
See drum-rhythm below

Drum-rhythm

Analysis.—A descending progression of a fourth constitutes almost 25 per cent of the intervals in this song. (See No. 3.) No rhythmic unit is present, although an eighth-note division is of frequent occurrence. The song is minor in tonality, melodic in structure, and lacks the second tone of the complete octave. The drumbeat was in quarter-note values, the strokes being of equal force.

No. 21. Sun Dance Song (d)　　　(Catalogue No. 777)

Recorded by SINGER No. 10

VOICE ♩= 88
DRUM ♩= 88
Drum-rhythm similar to No. 18

Analysis.—The rhythm of this song was accurately repeated in the three renditions except in the measure before the last, in which the note-values often were given as four eighth notes. The rhythmic form is irregular but coherent. Two rhythmic units occur, the first comprising one measure and the second nine measures. The song is minor in tonality, begins and ends on the dominant, and lacks the seventh and second tones of the complete octave. In structure it is melodic with harmonic framework, the tonic chord being strongly in evidence. Thirty-seven progressions occur, about two-thirds of which are descending intervals.

No. 22. Sun Dance Song (e)   (Catalogue No. 778)

Recorded by SINGER No. 10

VOICE ♪ = 132
DRUM ♪ = 132
Drum-rhythm similar to No. 18

Analysis.—Voice and drum have the same time unit in this song, the drum in unaccented eighth notes continuing steadily through the double and triple measures of the melody. The tonic chord is prominent in the structure of the song, which begins on the dominant in the upper octave and ends on the dominant in the lower octave. Only one other song (No. 72) of this series begins in 3–8 time.

No. 23. Sun Dance Song (f)   (Catalogue No. 710)

Recorded by SINGER No. 11

VOICE ♩ = 92
Drum not recorded

Analysis.—The tonic chord is prominent in the structure of this song, which, like the preceding song, begins and ends on the dominant. An unaccented half note occurs four times but does not form part of a rhythmic unit. Forty-three per cent of the progressions are semitones, a proportion which is unusual in analyzed Indian songs. This transcription is from the last of several renditions which show some slight points of difference.

No. 24. Sun Dance Song (g)   (Catalogue No. 786)

Recorded by SINGER No. 12

VOICE ♩= 88

DRUM ♩= 88

Drum-rhythm similar to No. 18

Analysis.—This song has a compass of 12 tones, which is somewhat unusual in Ute songs. A wide variety of progressions appear in the melody, but the only tones are those of the minor triad and fourth. The transcription is from the third of five renditions which show some unimportant variations.

No. 25. Sun Dance Song (h)   (Catalogue No. 787)

Recorded by SINGER No. 12

VOICE ♩= 88

Drum not recorded

Analysis.—This melody contains six sorts of ascending and six of descending intervals, which is an unusually wide variety. The tonic chord constitutes the framework of the melody, which contains all the tones of the octave except the seventh. Like several other Sun dance songs this begins on the dominant in the upper and ends on

the dominant in the lower octave.   The group of five sixteenth notes
was sung with distinctness.

No. 26. Sun Dance Song (i)   (Catalogue No. 798)

Recorded by SINGER No. 13

VOICE ♩ = 72
Drum not recorded

Analysis.—An aged woman recorded this song, which has a compass of an octave and contains the tones of the second five-toned scale. A sixteenth note followed by a dotted eighth note characterizes the melody, but does not form part of a rhythmic unit.

PLOTS OF SUN DANCE SONGS

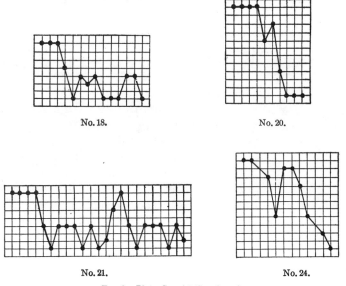

No. 18.   No. 20.

No. 21.   No. 24.

FIG. 2.—Plots, Group 2 (Sun dance)

A sharp descent characterizes the plots of the Sun dance songs, though in some instances (as in Nos. 18 and 21) this descent is followed by what has been termed the "horizontal type" of outline.

UNDETERMINED DANCE SONGS

The three songs next following were said to belong to a religious dance, the character of which was not determined.

No. 27. Undetermined Dance Song (a)   (Catalogue No. 788)

Recorded by SINGER No. 14

The words of this song were said to mean "On a mountain, the noise of the wind." These words were not recorded.

Analysis.—This melody is characterized by small progressions, 83 per cent of the intervals being a minor third, or smaller than a minor third—that is, containing from one to three semitones. The two rhythmic units have no resemblance to each other, one occurring in the first and the other in the latter portion of the song. The time values were given with exactness, three renditions being recorded and showing no differences. For other songs containing rests see No. 8. Only one other song of this series (No. 14) contains 5–8 measures.

No. 28. Undetermined Dance Song (b)   (Catalogue No. 789)

Recorded by SINGER No. 14

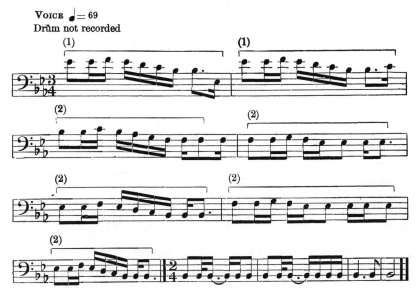

Analysis.—This song resembles the preceding in that it contains two rhythmic units and all the tones of the octave. About 89 per cent of the progressions are whole tones and semitones. Other songs containing a large proportion of these intervals are Nos. 34, 36, 41, 44, 49, 52, 73, 82, 89, 98, and 108. The song has a compass of 12 tones. The steadily descending trend of the melody is shown in the melody plot (fig. 2). This song and the song next following were recorded without drum, as no drum was used with them in the dance.

No. 29. Undetermined Dance Song (c)   (Catalogue No. 767)

Recorded by SINGER No. 5

Analysis.—The only intervals in this song are fourths and thirds, the major and minor thirds each constituting about 40 per cent of the entire number. Ascending and descending intervals are more nearly equal than in a majority of the songs under analysis. The repetitions of the rhythmic unit comprise the entire song except the opening and closing measures. All the tones of the octave, except the fourth, occur in the song, which has a compass of 10 tones. No change of time occurs in this melody.

SUN DANCE AND UNDETERMINED DANCE SONGS

MELODIC ANALYSIS

TABLE 1B.—TONALITY

	Number of songs	Serial Nos. of songs
Major tonality	6	22, 23, 25, 27, 28, 29.
Minor tonality	6	18, 19, 20, 21, 24, 26.
Total	12	

TABLE 2B.—FIRST NOTE OF SONG—ITS RELATION TO KEYNOTE

	Number of songs	Serial Nos. of songs
Beginning on the—		
Twelfth	2	20, 24.
Octave	3	18, 19, 28.
Fifth	6	21, 22, 23, 25, 26, 29.
Third	1	27.
Total	12	

TABLE 3B.—LAST NOTE OF SONG—ITS RELATION TO KEYNOTE

	Number of songs	Serial Nos. of songs
Ending on the—		
Fifth	7	21, 22, 25, 26, 27, 28, 29.
Keynote	5	18, 19, 20, 23, 24.
Total	12	

TABLE 4B.—LAST NOTE OF SONG—ITS RELATION TO COMPASS OF SONG

	Number of songs	Serial Nos. of songs
Songs in which final tone is lowest tone in song	10	18, 19, 20, 21, 23, 24, 25, 26, 27, 28.
Songs containing a minor third below the final tone	1	29.
Songs containing a whole tone below the final tone	1	22.
Total	12	

SUN DANCE AND UNDETERMINED DANCE SONGS—Continued

MELODIC ANALYSIS—continued

TABLE 5B.—NUMBER OF TONES COMPRISING COMPASS OF SONG

	Number of songs	Serial Nos. of songs
Compass of—		
Thirteen tones	1	23.
Twelve tones	3	20, 24, 28.
Ten tones	1	29.
Nine tones	2	19, 22.
Eight tones	5	18, 21, 25, 26, 27.
Total	12	

TABLE 6B.—TONE MATERIAL

	Number of songs	Serial Nos. of songs
Second five-toned scale	1	18.
Minor triad and fourth	1	24.
Octave complete	3	19, 27, 28.
Octave complete except seventh	3	22, 23, 25.
Octave complete except seventh and second	2	21, 26.
Octave complete except fourth	1	29.
Octave complete except second	1	20.
Total	12	

TABLE 7B.—ACCIDENTALS

	Number of songs	Serial Nos. of songs
Songs containing no accidentals	12	

TABLE 8B.—STRUCTURE

	Number of songs	Serial Nos. of songs
Melodic	3	18, 20, 29.
Melodic with harmonic framework	8	19, 21, 22, 23, 24, 25, 26, 28.
Harmonic	1	27.
Total	12	

TABLE 9B.—FIRST PROGRESSION—DOWNWARD AND UPWARD

	Number of songs	Serial Nos. of songs
Downward	8	18, 20, 21, 22, 24, 25, 26, 29.
Upward	4	19, 23, 27, 28.
Total	12	

SUN DANCE AND UNDETERMINED DANCE SONGS—Continued

MELODIC ANALYSIS—continued

TABLE 10B.—TOTAL NUMBER OF PROGRESSIONS—DOWNWARD AND UPWARD

	Number of songs	Serial Nos. of songs
Downward	224	
Upward	133	
Total	357	

TABLE 11B.—INTERVALS IN DOWNWARD PROGRESSION

	Number of songs	Serial Nos. of songs
Interval of a—		
Minor sixth	3	
Fifth	3	
Fourth	23	
Major third	14	
Minor third	53	
Major second	113	
Minor second	15	
Total	224	

TABLE 12B.—INTERVALS IN UPWARD PROGRESSION

	Number of songs	Serial Nos. of songs
Interval of—		
Octave	3	
Major sixth	2	
Minor sixth	3	
Fifth	6	
Fourth	22	
Major third	14	
Minor third	26	
Major second	50	
Minor second	7	
Total	133	

TABLE 13B.—AVERAGE NUMBER OF SEMITONES IN AN INTERVAL

Total number of intervals 357
Total number of semitones 1,095
Average number of semitones in an interval 3.06

SUN DANCE AND UNDETERMINED DANCE SONGS—Continued

MELODIC ANALYSIS—continued

TABLE 14B.—KEY

	Number of songs	Serial Nos. of songs
Key of—		
A major	1	25.
A minor	1	20.
B flat major	1	22.
B flat minor	3	19, 21, 26.
C minor	1	24.
E flat major	1	28.
G major	2	27, 29.
A flat major	1	23.
G sharp minor	1	18.
Total	12	

RHYTHMIC ANALYSIS

TABLE 15B.—PART OF MEASURE ON WHICH SONG BEGINS

	Number of songs	Serial Nos. of songs
Beginning on accented part of measure	10	18, 19, 20, 21, 22, 23, 25, 26, 28, 29.
Beginning on unaccented part of measure	2	24, 27.
Total	12	

TABLE 16B.—RHYTHM (METER) OF FIRST MEASURE

	Number of songs	Serial Nos. of songs
First measure in—		
2–4 time	6	18, 19, 20, 23, 27, 29.
3–4 time	5	21, 24, 25, 26, 28.
3–8 time	1	22.
Total	12	

TABLE 17B.—CHANGE OF TIME, MEASURE-LENGTHS

	Number of songs	Serial Nos. of songs
Songs containing no change of time	2	23, 29.
Songs containing a change of time	10	18, 19, 20, 21, 22, 24, 25, 26, 27, 28.
Total	12	

Sun Dance and Undetermined Dance Songs—Continued

RHYTHMIC ANALYSIS—continued

TABLE 18B.—RHYTHM (METER) OF DRUM

	Number of songs	Serial Nos. of songs
Eighth notes unaccented	5	19, 21, 22, 23, 24.
Quarter notes unaccented	1	20.
Drum not recorded	6	18, 25, 26, 27, 28, 29.
Total	12	

TABLE 19B.—RHYTHMIC UNIT OF SONG

	Number of songs	Serial Nos. of songs
Songs containing—		
No rhythmic units	4	18, 20, 25, 26.
One rhythmic unit	4	22, 23, 24, 29.
Two rhythmic units	4	19, 21, 27, 28.
Total	12	

TABLE 20B.—TIME UNIT OF VOICE

	Number of songs	Serial Nos. of songs
Metronome—		
69	1	28.
72	3	18, 19, 20.
76	1	23.
84	2	21, 27.
88	2	24, 25.
92	1	26.
104	1	29.
132	1	22.
Total	12	

TABLE 21B.—TIME UNIT OF DRUM

	Number of songs	Serial Nos. of songs
Metronome—		
72	2	19, 20.
76	1	23.
84	1	21.
88	1	24.
132	1	22.
Drum not recorded	6	18, 25, 26, 27, 28, 29.
Total	12	

SUN DANCE AND UNDETERMINED DANCE SONGS—Continued

RHYTHMIC ANALYSIS—continued

TABLE 22B.—COMPARISON OF TIME UNIT OF VOICE AND DRUM

	Number of songs	Serial Nos. of songs
Time unit of voice and drum the same...........................	6	19, 20, 21, 22, 23, 24.
Drum not recorded...	6	18, 25, 26, 27, 28, 29.
Total..	12	

SOCIAL DANCES OF LESS IMPORTANCE THAN THE BEAR DANCE

TURKEY DANCE

One of the principal dances of the Utes at the present time is known as the Turkey dance. This name was given the dance by white men, the native name meaning "jigging dance." The writer

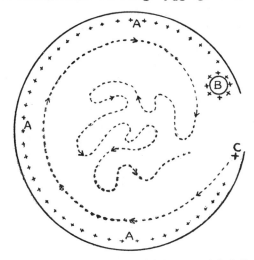

FIG. 3.—Diagram, Turkey dance. *a*, Dancing circle with dancers seated. *b*, Drum with drummers seated. *c*, Position of leader before dance begins. ------ Path taken by leader, who is followed by dancers. The erratic motion is continued indefinitely.

witnessed one of these dances in the summer of 1914. The accompanying instrument is a large drum placed on the ground at the right of the entrance to the dance circle, the drummers being seated around the drum and singing as they beat upon it. Women seldom participate in this dance. The motion of the dance is forward, and the step consists in putting the feet to the ground alternately, the point of the foot touching the ground first, after which the heel is "put down with an accent." There is no prescribed direction for the entrance of the dance circle. The drum, as already stated, is placed at the right of the entrance and the leader of the dancers sits at the left. In beginning the dance the leader rises and dances around the entire circle, the other dancers rising and following him. Having completed the round of the circle, he moves in an erratic manner, the dancers following close behind him (fig. 3). The dancers imitate a turkey by thrusting their heads forward and wagging them from side to side, while their arms hang loosely from the shoulders.

The Woman's dance is usually danced at the same time as the Turkey dance, these being the only two dances thus connected.

CHARACTERISTICS OF SONGS

An interrupted eighth-note drumbeat is the chief characteristic of these songs. This is transcribed with song No. 30 and was discernible in the phonograph records of the other songs. The rhythm of the voice shows a slight preference for 2–4 time and for beginning on the accented part of the measure. Melodically the songs are characterized by wide compass and small intervals of progression. Thus the compass of the songs is from 9 to 13 tones, and 93 per cent of the intervals are thirds and seconds. The average interval contains 2.8 semitones, and therefore is smaller than a minor third. The average interval in the entire series of Ute songs contains 3.14 semitones. (Table 13, p. 42.)

No. 30. Turkey Dance Song (a) (Catalogue No. 731)

Recorded by SINGER No. 7

VOICE $\quad \downarrow = 76$ ($\downarrow = 152$)
DRUM $\quad \downarrow = 76$ ($\downarrow = 152$)
Interrupted drum-rhythm as indicated

Analysis.—In this song the interrupted drumbeat, which characterizes the Turkey dance songs, was given with sufficient clearness to permit its transcription below the melody notes (cf. Nos. 31, 45).

25043°—22——7

The eighth-note values of the drumbeats were maintained more steadily in the 5–8 and 7–8 measures than in the 2–4 and 3–4 measures, and the drum was more synchronous with the voice in the latter than in the first part of the song; thus the notation of the drum should be understood as approximate rather than absolute. After singing the song as transcribed the singer began at the first measure without a break in the time, ending the performance with the ninth measure of the song. The third and sixth measures in both renditions were sung as indicated, although the ninth and eleventh measures from the close, containing the same progressions, were sung in 3–4 time.

Observing the formation of the melody, we note that it is major in tonality and comprises the tones of the fourth five-toned scale with B as keynote, yet the structure of the melody is chiefly that of the minor triad and seventh. (See analysis of No. 38.) The song has a compass of 11 tones, yet 87 per cent of the progressions contain two or three semitones.

No. 31. Turkey Dance Song (b)   (Catalogue No. 732)

Recorded by SINGER No. 7

VOICE ♩= 104
DRUM ♩= 104
Drum-rhythm similar to No. 30

Analysis.—This song resembles the preceding song in melodic structure, though differing widely from it in rhythm. Eighty-four per cent of the progressions contain two or three semitones, yet the song has a compass of 10 tones. Ascending and descending progressions are singularly uniform, there being in ascending progression 1 fourth, 3 minor thirds, and 3 major seconds, while the descending progressions comprise 2 fourths, 5 major thirds, and 5 major seconds. The tone material is that of the second five-toned scale. The interrupted drumbeat, noted in the preceding song, is present in this phonograph record but is not transcribed.

No. 32. Turkey Dance Song (c)　　　(Catalogue No. 741)

Recorded by SINGER No. 6

VOICE ♩ = 96

DRUM ♩ = 96
Drum-rhythm similar to No. 30

Analysis.—The downward trend of this song, following the intervals of the tonic chord, is emphasized by a glissando of the voice, indicated in the transcription. The melody contains only the tones of the major triad and second. It has a compass of 11 tones and a majority of the progressions are minor thirds. No ascending progressions occur between accented tones. (See plot, fig. 4.) Repetitions of the rhythmic unit comprise the entire melody except the closing measures.

No. 33. Turkey Dance Song (d)　　　(Catalogue No. 742)

Recorded by SINGER No. 6

VOICE ♩ = 80

DRUM ♩ = 88
Drum-rhythm similar to No 30

Analysis.—The progressions of this melody suggest E flat as a keynote, but G (the third) is not present and the melody is not classified in tonality or key. Another song of the present series lacking the third is No. 37. (See Bull. 53, p. 140, and Bull. 61, p. 135.) The interval of a fourth constitutes 22 per cent of the progressions, the remaining intervals, with one exception, being major and minor thirds. Two rhythmic periods comprise the entire song, a short rhythmic unit occurring in both periods. The drum is slightly faster than the voice and steadily maintained in the five renditions.

No. 34. Turkey Dance Song (e)   (Catalogue No. 790)
Recorded by Singer No. 15 (pl. 10, *a*)

Voice ♩ = 76

Drum ♩ = 76
Drum-rhythm similar to No. 30

Analysis.—In melodic structure this song comprises three parts: The first (3 measures) is based on the major triad B–D sharp–F sharp; the second (1 measure) on the minor triad G sharp–B–D sharp; and the third (4 measures) on the chord B–D sharp–F sharp–B, the accented tones following the descending intervals of this chord. The song is thus seen to be strongly harmonic in character. No interval larger than a minor third occurs in the song, and about 58 per cent of the progressions are whole tones. (See No. 28.) The song has a compass of 13 tones and contains the entire octave except the seventh. Repetitions of the rhythmic unit comprise practically the entire song.

No. 35. Turkey Dance Song (f)   (Catalogue No. 791)
Recorded by Singer No. 15

Voice ♩ = 72
Drum not recorded

Analysis.—This song is not rhythmic in character. It contains all the tones of the octave except the fourth and is harmonic in structure.

c, Pa'gitš

b, Kanav

a, Tsigu'p

a, To′pātšuk   *b*, Wiyu′tš

c, Charles Mack

About half the progressions are whole tones, but the ascending fifth occurs twice, giving interest to the song as a whole. Five renditions were recorded and show no points of difference.

PLOTS OF SONGS OF THE TURKEY DANCE

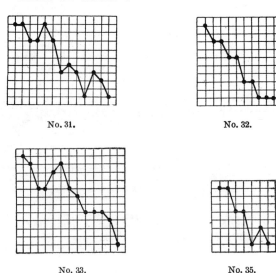

No. 31.　　　　　　　　　　　　　No. 32.

No. 33.　　　　　　　　　　　　　No. 35.

Fig. 4.—Plots, Group 3 (Turkey dance)

The plots of these songs show more uniformity than the plots of any other group of Ute songs. They are characterized chiefly by a sharply descending trend.

Woman's Dance

It was said that the Woman's dance was obtained by the Utes from the Shoshoni. As already stated, it was danced at the same time as the Turkey dance. Only three of its songs were recorded.

CHARACTERISTICS OF SONGS

The songs were accompanied by beating on a large drum. The drum rhythm is the same as that in songs of the Woman's dance recorded among the Chippewa. (See Bull. 45, p. 192.) It comprises an accented stroke and an unaccented stroke, the latter corresponding approximately to the third count of a triplet. A brief rest which separates these corresponds approximately to the second count of a triplet. In melodic compass these songs are smaller than the Turkey dance songs, and the progressions are larger. The largest range in any of these songs is nine tones, which was the smallest range in the Turkey songs, and 14 per cent of the intervals are a fourth, or larger than a fourth, as compared with 7 per cent of similar intervals in the Turkey dance songs.

No. 36. Woman's Dance Song (a)   (Catalogue No. 779)

Recorded by SINGER No. 10

VOICE ♩= 80

DRUM ♩= 80

See drum-rhythm below

Drum rhythm (approximate)

Analysis.—The rhythmic structure of this song is interesting. Two rhythmic units occur, the first containing three and the second two counts.   After a repetition of the first rhythmic unit we note a measure suggesting the second unit, followed by a measure resembling the first unit, this, in turn, followed by the second unit and its repetition.   The first unit reappears and is followed by a measure bearing resemblances to both units, the song closing with three repetitions of the second unit.   This intelligent use of thematic material indicates a degree of musical cultivation among the Utes. The melody has a compass of an octave and contains all the tones of the octave except the seventh.   Whole tones comprise 84 per cent of the progressions.   (See No. 28.)

No. 37. Woman's Dance Song (b)   (Catalogue No. 743)

Recorded by SINGER No. 6

VOICE ♩= 80

DRUM ♩= 80

Drum-rhythm similar to No. 36

Analysis.—This song contains the tones B flat, E flat, G natural, and A natural, suggesting the key of B flat major, yet the third of that key does not appear. (See No. 33.) The song begins with an ascending octave. Only one other Ute song has this initial interval (No. 91). Chippewa and Sioux songs with this peculiarity are noted in Bulletin 53, page 81, and Bulletin 61, page 343. It also begins and ends on the same tone. (See Nos. 42, 59, 91, and 97 of this series; also Bull. 53, p. 222, and Bull. 61, p. 257.) About one-third of the intervals are fourths. Two rhythmic units occur, the rhythm of the second unit being steadily different from that of the first unit. A first and second ending occurs also in the duplication No. 39 and in No. 48.

This song is considered in the Appendix, pages 206–208.

No. 38. Woman's Dance Song (c)   (Catalogue No. 744)

Recorded by SINGER No. 6

VOICE $\quad$ ♩ = 80

DRUM $\quad$ ♩ = 80

Drum-rhythm similar to No. 36

Analysis.—This song contains only the tones of the minor triad
and seventh.   The only other Ute song containing this tone material
is No. 71.

Concerning this characteristic among Chippewa songs, see Bulletin
45, page 142, and Bulletin 53, page 258; among the Sioux songs, see
Bulletin 61, pages 184, 337.   This chord has been found in the music of
the American Negro [18] and was noted by Prof. J. C. Fillmore in songs
of the Nass River Indians living in British Columbia; also among
the songs of the Dahomy collected by Prof. Fillmore at the World's
Columbian Exposition in Chicago, 1892.

In the songs analyzed by the present writer this chord appears in
two forms: (1) In songs of minor tonality it constitutes the tonic
chord with seventh added, and (2) in songs of major tonality it
constitutes the submediant chord with the dominant of the key
added as its highest tone.   It will be noted that in the first form
the tonic triad appears as the lower and in the second form as the
upper portion of the chord.   The second is the more frequent form,
as shown by the fact that 11 Chippewa songs are characterized by
this chord and only three are minor in tonality.   (See song No. 30.)
In the song under analysis the tonic triad (G sharp, B–D sharp)
forms the framework of the melody, the seventh being less prominent
and occurring only twice.   The rhythmic unit is short and its repetitions comprise all the song except the closing measures.   Four
renditions were recorded and show no differences except that in one
rendition the opening phrase, before the repeated portion, was
omitted.   Major and minor thirds constitute 68 per cent of the
progressions.

---

[18] See paper by H. E. Krehbiel, read before the Folklore Congress, July, 1894.

PLOTS OF SONGS OF THE WOMAN'S DANCE

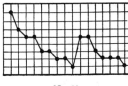
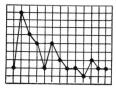

No. 36.   No. 37.

FIG. 5.—Plots, Group 4 (Woman's dance)

A comparison of the plots of these songs with the plots of the Turkey dance songs will show a more decided contrast than is evident to the ear in listening to the songs.

LAME DANCE

The action of the Lame dance was described as that of a man lame in the right leg. The motion was forward and the right foot was dragged as though it were crippled. This step, however, was entirely different from that of the Dragging-feet dance, in which the motion was sideways and the feet lifted clear of the ground. The steps of both of these were danced for the writer's observation, the dances themselves having fallen into disuse. Only women danced the Lame dance, and at a gathering in the old days it was not unusual for 100 women to take part in the dance. The women formed in two parallel lines more than 30 feet apart, standing one behind another, facing the west. Each line had its leader. At a considerable distance in front of these were the drummers, usually four in number, each with a hand drum, and behind the drummers was a line of men singers who faced the dancers. The women danced forward until near the drummers, when the leaders of the two lines turned and danced toward each other until they almost met. They then turned away from the drummers and danced side by side toward a point opposite that at which they started, the dancers following them and forming a double line (fig. 6).

CHARACTERISTICS OF SONGS

In all the Lame dance songs the accompanying drum is in quarter notes, following slightly after the voice. This does not appear in any other songs recorded among the Utes and may be considered a characteristic of the Lame dance. As in the Bear dance, the song used at the conclusion of the dance was different in structure from the other songs of the series. With the exception of the closing song (No. 42) a wide range obtains in the Lame dance songs, varying from 9 to 12 tones. With this wide range there occurs, as in the Turkey dance songs, a predominance of small intervals, 52 per cent

of the progressions being whole tones. The fourth is prominent,
comprising 12 per cent of the entire number of intervals. There is
a variety of tone-material in these songs, all of which are harmonic

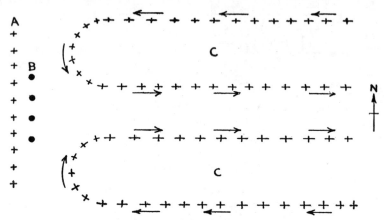

FIG. 6.—Diagram, Lame dance. *A*, Singers. *B*, Drummers. *C*, Path of dancers

in structure. The closing song contains only two tones, is simple in
rhythm, and has a drumbeat in unaccented eighth notes, the other
songs having a drumbeat in quarter notes. The accompanying
instrument was a hand drum.

No. 39. Lame Dance Song (a)   (Catalogue No. 701)

Recorded by SINGER No. 9

VOICE ♩ = 69

DRUM ♩ = 69

Drum-rhythm similar to No. 20

Analysis.—We have before us for consideration two renditions of a song by the same singer (cf. Nos. 77, 78), the first rendition being recorded in 1914 and the second in 1916. The duplication was accidental, which adds to the interest of the comparison. On the first occasion the song was sung three times and on the second it was sung twice. Comparing the transcriptions of the two renditions, we find in the second a more regular rhythm and also an ornamentation of the melody, as in the third measure. The first-named peculiarity is shown by the presence of rhythmic units, the latter by a larger proportion of whole-tone progressions. Inquiry was made concerning the life of the singer during the two years elapsing between the making of the records, as the rhythm might possibly be influenced by an adaptation to the ways of the white man. The Government officials on the reservation were, however, of the opinion that no appreciable change had taken place in the singer and the difference in the records was attributed by them to a difference in mood at the time of recording.

On comparing the analyses of the two renditions, we find the following resemblances and differences:

RESEMBLANCES

Tonality............................Major.
First tone...........................Octave.
Last tone...........................Fifth.
Compass............................12 tones.
Tone material.......................Octave complete except seventh.
Structure...........................Melodic.
First progression...................Upward.
Time of first measure...............2–4.

DIFFERENCES

	First rendition— Key of E major	Second rendition [1]— Key of E flat major
Number of progressions..................	31	47
Proportion of major thirds...	19	20
Proportion of major seconds..	40	58
Rhythmic unit...	None.	2
Time of voice and drum..	69	84

[1] Interesting features of the second rendition are the first and second endings and the connective phrase.

In both renditions the drum was in the same tempo as the voice, but was struck slightly after the corresponding tone of the voice. This appears to be a peculiarity of the Lame dance songs. In the comparison of the two renditions it appears that the resemblances are more important than the differences, establishing the identity of the song. A comparison of the plots, though not showing the rhythm of the song, indicates the greater regularity in the second rendition. Concerning the use of a connective phrase see No. 7. Syncopations (*nota legato*) occur also in songs Nos. 41 and 75. A first and second ending occurs also in Nos. 37 and 48.

This song is considered in the Appendix, pages 209–210.

Duplication of No. 39

Recorded by SINGER No. 9

Connective phrase between renditions

No. 40. Lame Dance Song (b)   (Catalogue No. 720)

Recorded by SINGER No. 16

VOICE ♩= 76
DRUM ♩= 76
Drum-rhythm similar to No. 20

Tši-yu-ta   Tši-yu-ta

Analysis.—This song contains only one word (Tšiyuta), said to be the Shoshoni term applied by them to the Utes.   The rhythmic structure of the song comprises four periods, each containing four measures, except the third, which has only three measures.   Each of these periods ends with a triple measure.   In melodic form the song is characterized by wide expansion and small intervals, the range being 11 tones and about 60 per cent of the progressions being smaller than a major third.   (See No. 28.)   Three renditions were recorded, the only differences being a slight variation in the fourth measure.   The song contains all the tones of the octave.

No. 41. Lame Dance Song (c)   (Catalogue No. 768)

Recorded by SINGER No. 17

VOICE ♩ = 63

DRUM ♩ = 63

Drum-rhythm similar to No. 20

Analysis.—Two renditions of this song were recorded, and in both are found the same number of sixteenth notes in the third measure from the close, this phrase being divided into three groups of two notes each. The song contains no rhythmic unit, though several measures begin with a dotted eighth followed by a sixteenth note. A short connective phrase was sung between the renditions. (See No. 7.) For other songs containing rests see analysis of No. 8. Sixty-five per cent of the progressions are whole tones—a peculiarity noted in the analysis of No. 28.

It was said that the following song was sung at the conclusion of the dance. A man approached a woman dancer and made a series of gestures, after which a third person threw a blanket over them, and they danced together while this song was sung.

No. 42. Closing song of the Lame Dance (Catalogue No. 769)

Recorded by SINGER No. 17

VOICE ♩= 104
DRUM ♩= 112
Drum-rhythm similar to No. 18

Analysis.—This song resembles No. 17, which was sung at the conclusion of the Bear dance, but a comparison of the trend of the two melodies shows the upper tone to be the more important in No. 17 and the lower tone in the present instance. A fundamental and its minor third are the only tones in this song, while No. 17 contains also the minor seventh, occurring as an unaccented tone. This song comprises four periods, all having the same rhythm. It begins and ends on the same tone. (See No. 37.)

PLOTS OF SONGS OF THE LAME DANCE

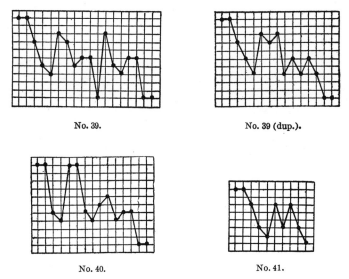

No. 39.   No. 39 (dup.).

No. 40.   No. 41.

FIG. 7.—Plots, Group 5 (Lame dance)

In the plot of these songs we have a type that appears to avoid the lowest point, differing in this respect from a majority of the Sioux as well as of the Ute songs.

The plots of No. 39 and also of its duplication are. shown, thus affording an opportunity for comparison which is clearer than that of the transcribed melodies.

DRAGGING-FEET DANCE

According to Star, an old informant, the Dragging-feet dance was one of the social dances held after a scalp dance. Men and women danced together, not alternating but standing as convenient, the motion of the dance being sideways, "with the sun." The step was that recorded in the same dance among other tribes (see Bull. 61, p. 477), one foot being advanced sideways and the other foot lifted and placed beside it.

CHARACTERISTICS OF SONGS

The drum beat with the Dragging-feet songs was in quarter notes, synchronous with the voice, not following after it, as in the Lame dance songs. Two of the songs contain particularly long rhythmic units, and none of the songs contain the seventh of the key. The minor fourth comprises 42 per cent and the fourth comprises 14 per cent of the entire number of intervals.

No. 43. Dragging-Feet Dance (a)   (Catalogue No. 721)

Recorded by SINGER No. 16

VOICE ♩ = 108
DRUM ♩ = 108
Drum-rhythm similar to No. 20

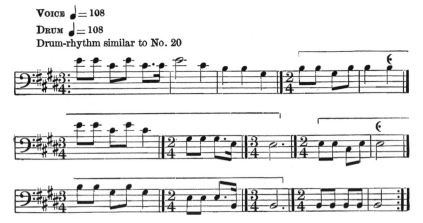

Analysis.—This melody progresses chiefly by the minor third, which constitutes 71 per cent of the intervals. The rhythmic unit comprises five measures and occurs twice. It is interesting to note the resemblance between the opening measures of the song and the rhythmic unit. Nine renditions were recorded without a break in the time. The drumbeat was synchronous with the voice.

No. 44. Dragging-Feet Dance (b)   (Catalogue No. 746)

Recorded by SINGER No. 18

VOICE $\quad\downarrow=104$
DRUM $\quad\downarrow=104$
Drum-rhythm similar to No. 20

Analysis.—Nine renditions of this song were recorded without a break in the time. The melody is rhythmic in character but contains no rhythmic unit. Only three sorts of progressions occur— the fourth (constituting 32 per cent), the major second (62 per cent), and one interval of a major third (see No. 28). All the major seconds were uncertain in intonation. The song is harmonic in structure and contains the octave complete except the second and seventh.

No. 45. Closing Song of the Dragging-Feet Dance

(Catalogue No. 702

Recorded by SINGER No. 9

VOICE $\quad\downarrow=104$
DRUM $\quad\downarrow=104$
Interrupted drum-rhythm as indicated

Analysis.—In this song, which was sung at the conclusion of the Dragging-feet dance, there was a break in the drumbeat, as a signal for the end of the dancing. This break was always given at the same point in the song. In two renditions this interruption occurred as

transcribed (cf. No. 30). It is interesting to note that in the interrupted portion the drumbeat is slightly after the voice, while in the
remainder of the song it is synchronous with the voice. The only
difference in the renditions (several of which were without drum) is
that in a few instances the first tone in the second occurrence of the
rhythmic unit was sung as a quarter note. The rhythmic unit is
long, as in No. 43. With the exception of one interval, a minor
sixth, the progressions are thirds and major seconds. The song is
melodic in structure and contains the tones of the fourth five-toned
scale.

PLOTS OF SONGS OF THE DRAGGING-FEET DANCE

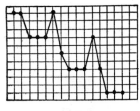   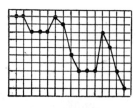

No. 43.   No. 45.

FIG. 8.—Plots, Group 6 (Dragging-feet dance)

The plots of these songs, while different from the plots of the Lame
dance songs, show a similar avoidance of the lowest point.

TEA DANCE

The name of the Tea dance indicates its modernness. If held outdoors the people danced around a fire, the men giving their bracelets
and other ornaments to the women who took part in the dance.

CHARACTERISTICS OF SONGS

A scanty tone-material and wide range characterize these songs,
none of which contain more than five degrees of the scale, while the
range of the songs is from 11 to 15 tones. Two are melodic in structure and one is melodic with harmonic framework, indicating freedom
of musical expression. The fourth, with its suggestion of motion
(see Bull. 53, p. 100), constitutes 28 per cent of the intervals. All
the songs are major in tonality, yet the minor third constitutes more
than 22 per cent of the progressions. The drumbeat of the dancing
song (No. 46) and of the song next following is similar to that of the
Woman's dance, the drumbeat of the third song being unaccented
eighth notes.

The following song was sung during the dancing:

No. 46. Tea Dance Song (a)   (Catalogue No. 733)

Recorded by SINGER No. 7

Analysis.—The keynote of this song is considered to be E, the tonality is therefore major, yet the major third appears only once as a progression. The interval of a fourth is strongly in evidence, both as a progression and in the structure òf the melody. A rhythmic unit occurs four times in succession, the two first occurrences being on the tone F sharp, E, B, and the second and third occurrences being on the tones B, G sharp, F sharp, after which the melody descends to B along lines which suggest the tonic chord. The portion of the melody included in measures 4 to 8 resembles numerous other Ute dances in its reiteration of a minor third (cf. Nos. 16, 42, 51). The tone material in this portion of the song is similar to that in No. 2. Other songs containing rests are noted in the analysis of No. 8, and other songs with connective phrase in the analysis of No. 7.

The two songs next following were sung after the people sat down and before the tea was served, a pipe being passed among them at this time.

No. 47. Tea Dance Song (b)   (Catalogue No. 734)

Recorded by SINGER No. 7

VOICE ♩ = 104

DRUM ♩ = 104
Drum-rhythm similar to No. 36

Analysis.—The drumbeat of this song is similar to that of the preceding song, during which the people danced. The song had the unusual range of 15 tones and is based on the fourth five-toned scale. Two renditions were recorded without variation. This is interesting, as three rhythmic units occur, the first and third closely resembling each other. The eighth measure contains a reversal of the count-divisions of the second rhythmic unit, in a triple measure. As has been noted, a measure of this sort frequently gives a certain balance to the rhythm of a song as a whole.

No. 48. Tea Dance Song (c)   (Catalogue No. 722)

Recorded by SINGER No. 16

VOICE ♩ = 84

DRUM ♩ = 84
Drum-rhythm similar to No. 18

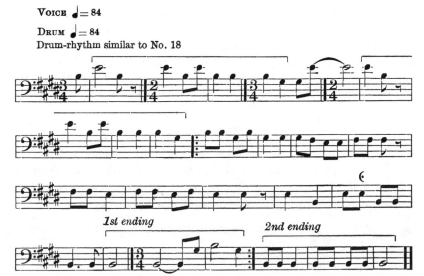

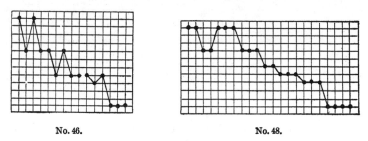

Analysis.—This song contains only the tones of the major triad and second, has a compass of 11 tones, and is melodic in structure. The fourth occurs 14 times, comprising about half the entire number of intervals. In contrast to the preceding song the drumbeat is in unaccented eighth notes. For other songs containing rests see No. 8. A first and second ending occurs also in the duplication of No. 39 and in No. 48.

PLOTS OF SONGS OF THE TEA DANCE

No. 46.   No. 48.

FIG. 9.—Plots, Group 7 (Tea dance)

A gentle descent characterizes the plots of these songs, with none of the activity noted in the two groups of dance songs next preceding it.

DOUBLE DANCE [19]

Both men and women danced the Double dance, which was said to be very old. The dancers stood in two lines facing each other and not far apart. Men and women did not alternate in these lines, but stood in any convenient order. So general was the interest in this dance that in old times the lines often were 30 or 40 feet long. In the dance one line moved forward about four steps, the opposite line receding. The opposite line then advanced and the first line receded.

CHARACTERISTICS OF SONGS

Two songs of this dance were recorded by Uncompahgre Utes. Both songs have a clear rhythmic structure with more than one rhythmic unit. No progression larger than a fourth occurs in these songs. The accompanying instrument was a hand drum.

No. 49. Double Dance Song (a)   (Catalogue No. 776)

Recorded by SINGER No. 8

VOICE ♩ = 112
DRUM ♩ = 112
Drum-rhythm similar to No. 20

Analysis.—A progression by whole tones characterizes this melody, about 73 per cent of the intervals being major seconds. (See No. 28.) Two rhythmic units occur—one in double, the other in triple time. These differ in the latter portion. The song is based on the second five-toned scale and has a compass of six tones. Drum and voice are synchronous.

---

[19] Nawa'to, a term used with reference to anything that is "doubled together."

No. 50. Double Dance Song (b)　　　(Catalogue No. 770)

Recorded by SINGER No. 17

VOICE ♩ = 92

DRUM ♩ = 92

Drum-rhythm similar to No. 18

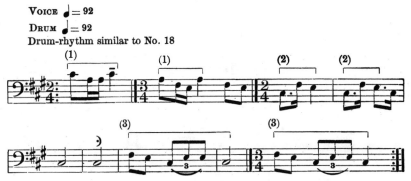

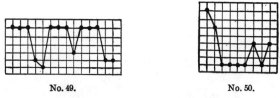

Analysis.—This song comprises three rhythmic periods, each with its rhythmic unit. The tone material is the major triad and sixth, which is less frequent in the Ute songs than in those of the Chippewa and Sioux. An ascending fourth occurs five times and a descending minor third occurs nine times. In contrast to the preceding song the drumbeat is in unaccented eighth notes.

PLOTS OF SONGS OF THE DOUBLE DANCE

No. 49.　　　　　　　　No. 50.

FIG. 10.—Plots, Group 8 (Double dance)

In these plots there appears a "horizontal type" of outline with rather wide intervals, the melody seeming to be "doubled" on itself rather than following a decided trend, as, for instance, in the songs of the Turkey dance.

IRON LINE DANCE

This is an old dance, in which both men and women participated, standing alternately in the dancing circle. In the step of this dance one foot was passed either over or behind the other and placed flat on the ground. The motion of the dance was sideways, the dancers progressing "with the sun." All the dancers sang and some of the men carried hand drums, with which they accompanied the singing.

No. 51. Iron Line Dance Song   (Catalogue No. 703)

Recorded by SINGER No. 9

Pi - nu - pi - ya

pi - nu - pi - ya

WORDS

pinu′piya..................second wife.

Analysis.—Two rhythmic units occur in this song, the second appearing to be an elaboration of the first. The opening and closing measures contain phrases which resemble but do not repeat the rhythmic unit. The principal interval is the minor third, which constitutes more than 60 per cent of the progressions. All the tones of the octave occur in the song, which is harmonic in structure. Drum and voice are synchronous.

PLOT OF SONG OF THE IRON LINE DANCE

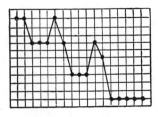

No. 50.

FIG. 11.—Plot, Group 9 (Iron Line dance

The plot of this melody is strong and interesting but of no definite type.

SOCIAL DANCE SONGS

MELODIC ANALYSIS

TABLE 1C.—TONALITY

	Number of songs	Serial Nos. of songs
Major tonality...	16	30, 32, 34, 35, 36, 39, 40, 41, 43, 44, 45, 46, 47, 48, 50, 51.
Minor tonality...	4	31, 38, 42, 49.
Third lacking...	2	33, 37.
Total..	22	

TABLE 2C.—FIRST NOTE OF SONG—ITS RELATION TO KEYNOTE

	Number of songs	Serial Nos. of songs
Beginning on the—		
Twelfth...	1	34.
Tenth...	2	31, 45.
Ninth...	1	46.
Octave...	9	35, 36, 39, 40, 41, 43, 47, 48, 51.
Fifth...	3	31, 37, 38.
Third...	2	32, 50.
Second...	1	33.
Keynote...	3	42, 44, 49.
Total..	22	

TABLE 3C.—LAST NOTE OF SONG—ITS RELATION TO KEYNOTE

	Number of songs	Serial Nos. of songs
Ending on the—		
Fifth...	11	33, 37, 38, 39, 40, 43, 44, 46, 48, 49, 51.
Third...	4	30, 32, 47, 50.
Keynote...	7	31, 34, 35, 36, 41, 42, 45.
Total..	22	

SOCIAL DANCE SONGS—Continued

MELODIC ANALYSIS—continued

TABLE 4C.—LAST NOTE OF SONG—ITS RELATION TO COMPASS OF SONG

	Number of songs	Serial Nos. of songs
Songs in which final tone is—		
Lowest tone in song	14	30, 31, 33, 34, 36, 39, 40, 41, 42, 43, 45, 46, 48, 50.
Immediately preceded by—		
Major third below	1	38.
Minor third below	1	51.
Whole tone below	3	32, 44, 47.
Semitone below	1	35.
Songs containing a major third below the final tone	1	49.
Songs containing a semitone below the final tone	1	37.
Total	22	

TABLE 5C.—NUMBER OF TONES COMPRISING COMPASS OF SONG

	Number of songs	Serial Nos. of songs
Compass of—		
Fifteen tones	1	47.
Thirteen tones	1	34.
Twelve tones	3	33, 39, 46.
Eleven tones	6	30, 32, 40, 43, 48, 51.
Ten tones	3	31, 38, 45.
Nine tones	3	35, 37, 41.
Eight tones	2	36, 50.
Seven tones	1	44.
Six tones	1	49.
Three tones	1	42.
Total	22	

TABLE 6C.—TONE MATERIAL

	Number of songs	Serial Nos. of songs
Second five-toned scale	2	31, 49.
Fourth five-toned scale	4	30, 41, 45, 47.
Major triad and sixth	1	50.
Major triad and second	3	32, 46, 48.
Minor triad and seventh	1	38.
Octave complete	2	40, 51.
Octave complete except seventh	3	34, 36, 39.
Octave complete except seventh and sixth	1	44.
Octave complete except seventh and third	1	33.
Octave complete except seventh and second	1	43.
Octave complete except fourth	1	35.
Octave complete except third	1	37.
Minor third	1	42.
Total	22	

SOCIAL DANCE SONGS—Continued

MELODIC ANALYSIS—continued

TABLE 7C.—ACCIDENTALS

	Number of songs	Serial Nos. of songs
Songs containing no accidentals.................................	22	

TABLE 8C.—STRUCTURE

	Number of songs	Serial Nos. of songs
Melodic...	11	31, 33, 36, 37, 39, 40, 41. 45, 46, 48, 49.
Melodic with harmonic framework............................	3	30, 38, 47.
Harmonic...	8	32, 34, 35, 42, 43, 44, 50, 51.
Total..	22	

TABLE 9C.—FIRST PROGRESSION—DOWNWARD AND UPWARD

	Number of songs	Serial Nos. of songs
Downward...	14	31, 33, 35, 36, 38, 40, 43, 45, 46, 47, 48, 49, 50, 51.
Upward...	8	31, 32, 34, 37, 39, 41, 42, 44.
Total..	22	

TABLE 10C.—TOTAL NUMBER OF PROGRESSIONS—DOWNWARD AND UPWARD

	Number of songs	Serial Nos. of songs
Downward...	420	
Upward...	248	
Total..	668	

TABLE 11C.—INTERVALS IN DOWNWARD PROGRESSION

	Number of songs	Serial Nos. of songs
Interval of a—		
Fourth..	50	
Major third...	29	
Minor third...	140	
Major second..	190	
Minor second..	11	
Total..	420	

Social Dance Songs—Continued

MELODIC ANALYSIS—continued

TABLE 12C.—INTERVALS IN UPWARD PROGRESSION

	Number of songs	Serial Nos. of songs
Interval of a—		
Ninth	1	
Octave	3	
Seventh	1	
Major sixth	2	
Minor sixth	6	
Fifth	10	
Fourth	35	
Major third	26	
Minor third	78	
Major second	84	
Minor second	2	
Total	248	

TABLE 13C.—AVERAGE NUMBER OF SEMITONES IN AN INTERVAL

Total number of intervals 668
Total number of semitones 1,657
Average number of semitones in an interval 2.4

TABLE 14C.—KEY

	Number of songs	Serial Nos. of songs
Key of—		
A major	1	50.
B flat major	2	36, 45.
B major	3	30, 32, 34.
B minor	1	49.
D flat major	1	44.
D major	1	51.
E major	7	35, 39, 40, 41, 43, 46, 48.
F sharp minor	1	31.
G major	1	47.
G sharp minor	2	38, 42.
Third lacking	2	33, 37.
Total	22	

RHYTHMIC ANALYSIS

TABLE 15C.—PART OF MEASURE ON WHICH SONG BEGINS

	Number of songs	Serial Nos. of songs
Beginning on unaccented part of measure	6	32, 35, 38, 44, 46, 48.
Beginning on accented part of measure	16	30, 31, 33, 34, 36, 37, 39, 40, 41, 42, 43, 45, 47, 49, 50, 51.
Total	22	

Social Dance Songs—Continued

RHYTHMIC ANALYSIS—continued

TABLE 16c.—RHYTHM (METER) OF FIRST MEASURE

	Number of songs	Serial Nos. of songs
First measure in—		
2–4	13	30, 31, 32, 35, 36, 37, 39, 40, 42, 44, 46, 47.
3–4	9	33, 34, 38, 41, 43, 45, 48, 49, 50, 51.
Total	22	

TABLE 17c.—CHANGE OF TIME, MEASURE-LENGTHS

	Number of songs	Serial Nos. of songs
Songs containing no change of time	3	32, 34, 42.
Songs containing a change of time	19	30, 31, 33, 35, 36, 37, 38, 39, 40, 41, 43, 44, 45, 46, 47, 48, 49, 50, 51.
Total	22	

TABLE 18c.—RHYTHM (METER) OF DRUM

	Number of songs	Serial Nos. of songs
Eighth notes unaccented	7	30, 31, 32, 33, 42, 48, 50.
Quarter notes unaccented	8	39, 40, 42, 43, 44, 45, 49, 51.
Each beat preceded by an unaccented beat corresponding to third count of a triplet	5	36, 37, 38, 46, 47.
Drum not recorded	2	34, 35.
Total	22	

TABLE 19c.—RHYTHMIC UNIT OF SONG

	Number of songs	Serial Nos. of songs
Songs containing—		
No rhythmic units	5	30, 35, 39, 41, 44.
One rhythmic unit	12	31, 32, 33, 34, 38, 40, 42, 43, 45, 46, 48, 49.
Two rhythmic units	3	36, 37, 51.
Three rhythmic units	2	47, 50.
Total	22	

Social Dance Songs—Continued

RHYTHMIC ANALYSIS—continued

TABLE 20c.—TIME UNIT OF VOICE (AT BEGINNING OF SONG)

	Number of songs	Serial Nos. of songs
Metronome—		
63	1	41.
69	1	36.
72	1	35.
76	3	30, 34, 40.
80	4	33, 36, 37, 38.
84	1	48.
88	1	46.
92	1	50.
96	1	32.
104	5	31, 42, 44, 45, 47.
108	1	43.
112	1	49.
116	1	51.
Total	22	

TABLE 21c.—TIME UNIT OF DRUM

	Number of songs	Serial Nos. of songs
Metronome—		
63	1	41.
69	1	39.
76	2	30, 40.
80	3	36, 37, 38.
84	1	48.
88	2	33, 46.
92	1	50.
96	1	32.
104	4	31, 44, 45, 47.
108	1	43.
112	2	42, 49.
116	1	51.
Drum not recorded	2	34, 35.
Total	22	

TABLE 22c.—COMPARISON OF TIME UNIT OF VOICE AND DRUM

	Number of songs	Serial Nos. of songs
Time unit of voice and drum the same	18	30, 31, 32, 36, 37, 38, 39, 40, 41, 43, 44, 45, 46, 47, 48, 49, 50, 51.
Voice slower than drum	2	33, 42.
Drum not recorded	2	34, 35.
Total	22	

TREATMENT OF THE SICK

Two native methods of treating the sick were in use among the Utes at the time this material was in preparation (1914–1916). In both these methods there was a dependence on supernatural aid, but in one method no material means were employed, while in the other method it was customary to administer herbs or other remedies. These two methods were also used by the Chippewa and Sioux,[20] and following the precedent of those volumes the term "medicine man" will be used to designate the person who depended entirely upon supernatural means and the term "doctor" to designate the person administering herbs. The following section comprises information given by Pa′gitš (pl. 10, c), a representative of the first-named method, and Mrs. Washington, a representative of the second. Pa′gitš explained the distinction between the two methods by saying that a medicine man, when treating a sick person, proceeded according to directions from his supernatural adviser, given him at the time, while a doctor, under similar circumstances, stated first the authority by which he practiced his profession, describing a long-past vision, usually of a bird or animal. · He said that medicine men did not buy songs of each other, as every medicine man possessed the ability to secure songs in a supernatural manner. Doctors, on the other hand, were accustomed to buy and sell songs, the older doctors frequently transferring songs to younger men. A good remedy was worth a horse, this price including the herb, the history of its medicinal use, and the song without which it would not be effective.

Pa′gitš, whose material will first be presented, said that he was entirely independent of material means, not even using a rattle or wearing amulets or "charms" when treating the sick. He said that after seeing and questioning a sick person he could tell whether he could cure him. On being asked whether he ever began the treatment of a case concerning which he felt uncertain, he replied without hesitation that he never did so, saying, "We believe that if a doctor begins on a case which he is not sure he can cure he will certainly fail." Continuing, he said, "I always tell the person that he will get well because I *know it is true;*" also, "If the sick person does not think I can cure him I do not talk about it; I just cure him and prove it." [21]

Concerning the source of his power, Pa′gitš said that he treated the sick under the tutelage of a "little green man" and that numerous

---

[20] Bull. 45, Bur. Amer. Ethn., pp. 119–124; Bull. 61, Bur. Amer. Ethn., pp. 244–278.

[21] These statements are given in the words of the interpreter. Care was taken that the form of a question did not suggest a possible answer, there being no desire to demonstrate the existence of mental treatment among Indians.

other medicine men were under the same guidance, there being many of the little green men. He first saw the little green man when he was. a boy of about 12 years and has seen him at intervals ever since. The songs used in his treatment of the sick were, however, received by him about three years previous to giving this information. At that time he was in the mountains and fell asleep. He then heard the little green man singing these songs and learned them in this manner. He said that when a man hears a song in a dream he sings aloud in his sleep and remembers the song after he wakes. (See p. 60.)

Describing the "little green man," Pa'gitš indicated his height as about 2 feet, saying he was green from head to foot and carried a bow and arrows. In disposition he was "good to those he liked," and especially favored medicine men. He could hear those who spoke unkindly of him and "shot his arrow" into them. These "arrows" were removed by the medicine men, who were paid for the treatment.

Pa'gitš said that the little green man "came around only at night." If Pa'gitš wished to talk with the little green man he sat outdoors in the early morning before sunrise. He sat facing the east and smoked. No ceremonial act was connected with this and he had no drum or rattle, neither did he sing. Sometimes it was not even necessary for him to smoke in order to talk with the little green man. If he wished to make a present to the little green man he left it beside the "hole" which was the door of his dwelling. He was not obliged to give him a present after each successful treatment of the sick, but once in a while he gave him a handkerchief or other small gift.

The abodes of the little green men were said to look like little chimneys and to be scattered through the mountains or any unsettled country. Those who pass such a dwelling and recognize it always throw a little branch of cedar or some other offering in front of it so the little man will not be angry with them. Tradition says that one night some white people filled the door of a little green man's house with stones, but in the morning all the stones had been removed. Pa'gitš said: "The little man makes a fire at night, and you can see a little light. In the early morning you can see smoke coming out of his house."

Those who summoned Pa'gitš to treat a sick person brought with them a stick about 18 inches long, painted green and forked at the end. This was his particular token and he made one for the writer. When he reached the abode of the sick person he was directed by the little green man as to what he should do. He always questioned the sick person about what he had been doing, with a view to ascertaining the cause of his distress. It might be due to a physical ailment, or (what was an entirely different matter) his distress might be due to "poisoning." Thus it was said that "a person who had a bad plant could put it in a man's footprints and poison him." In that case it was the duty of the medicine man to learn who had poisoned his patient and to counteract it. Thus he would say to the sick man: "I dreamed so and so, and I know who or what has poisoned you." Pa'gitš said that throughout his treatments the little green man stayed outside the tent, and he could see him and hear what he said, every phase of the treatment being according to his direction.

Nine "medicine songs" were recorded by Pa'gitš, who said that he sang them all when treating the sick. The relatives of those whom he frequently treated had learned these songs and sang them with him, continuing their singing when the method of treatment required that he place his head against the body of the patient. Pa'gitš' "specialty" was the treatment of acute pain, and he said that he could cure pain in any part of the body. He said that he took from the patient's body a "strange something," sucking it out through the skin. Then he took it from his mouth, held it in his hand, and showed it to all the people, after which he put it again in his mouth. As soon as this substance was removed from the patient's body he began to recover. Sometimes this substance is one of the little green man's arrows which he has shot into the person's body. In shape this "strange something" was said to be "like a carrot" and 1 or 2 inches in length. In color it was red, like blood, and in texture it was not unlike a fingernail. The "arrows" were always of the same kind, differing only in size. Pa'gitš said that he usually had to sing five times before he could extract this cause of the pain from his patient's body. He sings five times in one evening, cures the patient, and receives "about five or six dollars" as compensation. When he has sung for some time he says to the people around him, "Sing harder, sing harder; I am going to take out what causes the pain." In a few moments he has it in his hand and shows it to them all.[22]

In describing the treatment of general cases by medicine men, Pa'gitš said that it often took two or three weeks to cure a sick person, the medicine man singing at first every evening and then less often as the condition of the patient improved. Sometimes he sang two hours at a time, and if the person were very ill the medicine man would continue his singing until daylight. "If the medicine men are afraid a person will die, they pray and talk a great deal to his spirit."

The second group of songs in this section were recorded by a woman known as Mrs. Washington, who considered that she treated

---

[22] Fred Mart, the writer's interpreter, stated that he once saw a treatment similar to that described by Pa'gitš and saw the substance apparently removed from the person's body. It was red, about an inch long, and shaped like an arrow point.

the sick by the aid of supernatural power but who gave herb medicines in connection with the treatment. She said that she usually sang these songs when the sun was at a height corresponding to about 10 o'clock in the morning. The special efficacy of her songs was said to consist in their power to counteract an evil influence produced by some other person.

Mrs. Washington had been treating the sick for about four years prior to the recording of her songs and said that "a spirit" told her what to do. This spirit was represented by an eagle. In summoning her to treat a sick person, the messenger formerly brought a tail feather of an eagle, but recently she had required that he bring a downy white eagle feather, as she believed that her power was increased by this feather. If she were not at home, the messenger left the feather, on which there was no mark of any kind. Her friends told her who required her services and when she received the message she went at once to the sick person, taking with her the feather which had accompanied the request. She also held this feather in her hand during the treatment. Arrived at the home of the sick person, she "prayed to the eagle" before beginning her treatment, which was described as follows: The sick person was placed in a reclining position and she sat beside him, placing her forehead against that portion of his body where pain was felt. Sometimes she took earth and rubbed it on the patient's body, "working downward toward the feet." This earth was not prepared in any way but was used "just as it was picked up." During this treatment she sang the six recorded songs in the order in which they are herewith presented. If the patient were very ill, she used a plant which she obtained from the Shoshoni, but she valued this so highly that she used it only for those who were closely related to her. She stated that by means of this plant she once cured her daughter, who was almost in a dying condition. No specimen of the plant was available for identification, but the woman stated that she used the root in powdered form and also had "three little round red things," which were part of the plant. These were said to resemble a walnut but were smoother than a walnut and red in color. They were pierced with a hole so that they resembled large beads. The sick person was required to place one of these in his mouth and "draw air through the hole." This was used with all her medicinal herbs. The roots of various herbs were used by her in her treatment. These roots were powdered and prepared with water, the mixture being administered by dipping a "little stick" in it and applying the stick to the patient's tongue. As she gave the herb medicine she "prayed to the eagle." She said that when this treatment was administered the patient was sure to recover.

CHARACTERISTICS OF SONGS

In the tabulated analysis of these songs (p. 141) we note that two-thirds are major in tonality—a characteristic which is commonly associated with cheerfulness. The upward tendency of the melodies is shown by the fact that only two of the songs begin on an interval higher than the fifth, and yet 13 of the songs have a compass of more than five tones. This compass could only be attained by an ascent above the initial tone. This is a contrast to a large proportion of songs analyzed in which the first tone is the highest occurring in the melody. The melodic material is scanty. Eleven of the 15 songs contain four or less scale-degrees, three are on a five-toned scale, and one contains the octave complete except the sixth and seventh. None of the songs are harmonic in structure and a large majority are purely melodic. Two-thirds of the songs begin with an upward progression, and 60 per cent of the entire number of intervals are ascending intervals. The average interval contains 2.9 semitones. This is also the average interval in the songs of the Chippewa Mïde', whose fundamental idea is somewhat parallel to that represented by these songs. As stated in a previous work (Bull. 45, p. 13), "the Mïde' (Grand Medicine) is the native religion of the Chippewa * * *. Its chief aim is to secure health and long life to its adherents, and music forms an essential part of every means used to that end." Also (p. 20), "The power of the Mïde' is exerted through a combination of two mediums, music and medicine."

Observing the rhythmic characteristics of this group, we find that four-fifths of the songs begin with an upward interval and contain a 2–4 division in the first measure. This occurred also in 42 per cent of the Chippewa Mïde' songs and in 55 per cent of the Sioux songs used in treating the sick. (Cf. in this connection Bull. 53, p. 10.) All the songs contain a change of time. This occurs in all but one of the similar songs and in about three-fourths of the Mïde' songs. Fourteen of these songs have one or more rhythmic units, all but one of the Sioux songs containing such units and 87 per cent of the Mïde' songs having the same peculiarity. These songs were sung slower than similar songs among the other tribes mentioned.

Summary.—From these comparisons it is found that songs used in the treatment of the sick among the three tribes analyzed have more resemblance to each other than to other groups of songs, suggesting a correspondence between the content of the song and the form of its musical expression.

No. 52. Song used in treatment of sick (a)

(Catalogue No. 711)

Recorded by SINGER No. 11

♩ = 58
Drum not recorded

No. 53. Song used in treatment of sick (b)

(Catalogue No. 712)

Recorded by SINGER No. 11

♩ = 58
Drum not recorded

No. 54. Song used in treatment of sick (c)

(Catalogue No. 713)

Recorded by SINGER No. 11

♩ = 76
Drum not recorded

No. 55. Song used in treatment of sick (d)

(Catalogue No. 714)

Recorded by SINGER No. 11

♩ = 58
Drum not recorded

No. 56. Song used in treatment of sick (e)

(Catalogue No. 715)

Recorded by SINGER No. 11

♩ = 76
Drum not recorded

No. 57. Song used in treatment of sick (f)

(Catalogue No. 716)

Recorded by SINGER No. 11

♩ = 58
Drum not recorded

No. 58. Song used in treatment of sick (g)

(Catalogue No. 717)

Recorded by SINGER No. 11

♩ = 58
Drum not recorded

No. 59. Song used in treatment of sick (h)

(Catalogue No. 718)

Recorded by SINGER No. 11

♩ = 58
Drum not recorded

No. 60. Song used in treatment of sick (i)

(Catalogue No. 719)

Recorded by SINGER No. 11

♩ = 63
Drum not recorded

SONGS NOS. 52–60

Analysis.—These songs were repeated with less accuracy than any previously recorded by the writer, yet they differ from the "rudimentary songs" (pp. 200–205) in that each song, as transcribed, was found to occur at least twice on the phonograph cylinder. Each of these songs has a definite beginning and ending, the remainder of the cylinder containing melodic and rhythmic phrases which resemble but do not duplicate those of the song. It can scarcely be stated with positiveness whether these performances represent songs which are only partially separated from the thematic material of which they are made (see analysis of rudimentary songs) or are an intentional "breaking up" of composed songs. That the latter is a correct inference is suggested by three observations: (1) These songs were the personal property of the singer, and it would not be to his interest to repeat them so accurately that others could learn them. (2) The singer was a medicine man, and with the element of mystery surrounding his performance it would suit his purpose to present an "identity with variety" in his songs. He said the people "sang with him." As each song has an easily learned unit of rhythm, it would be quite possible for him to lead the people through a succession of simple melodic progressions, depending chiefly on the recurrent rhythm for their interest. (3) The personal equation of the singer should be taken into account. The man who recorded these songs was a comparatively young man, well built, keen-eyed, and apparently master of himself. The rudimentary songs were recorded by aged women.

It is interesting to note in this connection the pitch of these phonograph records. The uniformity of pitch in successive songs suggests mental concentration and among musicians of the white race would be considered an evidence of musical ability. Consideration should also be given to the fact that the interpreter used the word "song" in reference to these, suggesting that to his mind they had an identity. The rudimentary songs were interpreted by a different person, but the word "song" was modified, the interpreter saying "They sing this way when they tell stories."

As a melodic peculiarity of these songs we note the sequence of "keys" in the musicians' use of that term. (See tabulated statement below.) It may seem anomalous to apply the term "key" to these songs, as in almost half of them the third above the (apparent) keynote does not occur. However, by applying this broad test, we find what appears to be a connection between the idea of these songs and their melodic content. The idea underlying the songs was a desire that a sick person should recover, and in the sequence of tone material or "keys," we find an effect of uncertainty followed by an effect of confidence and rejoicing. The singer's intonation was fairly accurate throughout the songs, especially on what may be termed the boundaries of the melody. Thus B flat, which is the opening tone of the first six songs (Nos. 52–57), was unmistakable; also F and E flat, occurring later in the songs; while the B natural in the last three songs was given with similar distinctness. The tone material of the songs is as follows:

No. of song	Keynote	Degrees of major diatonic scale occurring in song
52	E flat.....	1,2,3,5,6.[1]
53	...do.......	1,2,5.
54	...do.......	1,2,3,5.
55	B flat.....	1,2,5,6.
56	...do.......	1,2,5,6.
57	...do.......	1,2,5,6.
58	...do.......	1,2,3,5.
59	...do.......	1,2,3,5,6.
60	...do.......	1,2,3,5,6.

[1] Fourth five-toned scale.

Since we are accustomed to hearing tuned instruments, the effect of this sequence of tone material can probably be noted most clearly by playing the tones on a piano. This will be the more evident if the chords of E flat, B flat, and G major are sounded before the single tones used in the melody are played. The singer said that at a certain point in his performance he told the people to "sing harder," as he was about to extract the cause of the pain.   It appears possible that this may have occurred at about the seventh song (No. 58).

In two-thirds of this group of songs the first progression is upward, and in a similar number the song begins on the accented portion of the measure, both of these features suggesting confidence.   The melodic progressions consist chiefly of fourths and major seconds.   It has been frequently noted in Sioux and Chippewa songs that the interval of a fourth characterizes songs concerning motion.   It is a progression of freedom, and does not suggest the feeling of certainty which characterizes the perfect fifth or the major third.   We note that the fourth occurs 53 times in these songs, while the perfect fifth occurs but once. The fourth constitutes 19 per cent of the entire number of intervals and the major second constitutes 66 per cent.   (See No. 24.)   The latter interval is seldom used as a passing tone, but alternates with the tone below it in a manner which is without melodic importance. The major third occurs only in Nos. 52, 54, and 60, and constitutes about 4 per cent of the intervals.   The songs are freely melodic in structure.

Turning to the rhythm of the songs, we find that with one exception the songs contain a rhythmic unit, and that there is a greater variety in the rhythmic units than in the melodic form of the songs. Except in No. 60 the rhythmic unit occurs only twice in a melody, but portions of it appear throughout the song, indicating that this phrase has a constructive influence on the form of the entire song.

No. 61. Song used in treatment of sick (j)

(Catalogue No. 752)

Recorded by SINGER No. 25

No. 62. Song used in treatment of sick (k)

(Catalogue No. 753)

Recorded by SINGER No. 25

No. 63. Song used in treatment of sick (l)

(Catalogue No. 754)

Recorded by SINGER No. 25

No. 64. Song used in treatment of sick (m)

(Catalogue No. 755)

Recorded by SINGER No. 25

No. 65. Song used in treatment of sick (n)

(Catalogue No. 756)

Recorded by SINGER No. 25

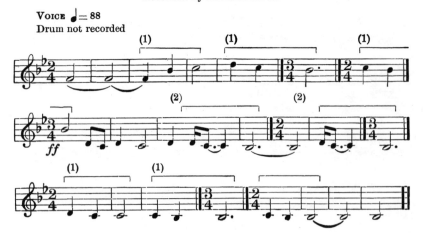

No. 66. Song used in treatment of sick (o)

Recorded by Singer No. 25

(Catalogue No. 757)

Voice ♩ = 66
Drum not recorded

SONGS NOS. 61–66

Analysis.—These songs will be analyzed collectively, since, like the preceding group, they are the property of an individual and all pertain to one subject. In the preceding group a majority of the songs are major in tonality and begin with an upward progression. In this group of six songs five are major in tonality and four begin with an ascending interval. The keynote is the final tone in all the songs. Five begin with a 2–4 measure-division, a peculiarity which occurred in seven of the nine songs in the previous group recorded by Pa′gitš. None are harmonic in structure, though in four songs there is an evident harmonic feeling. It is interesting to note that the first three songs are in tempo ♩ = 58, which was the tempo of two-thirds of Pa′gitš's songs. These, like his, are characterized by the interval of a fourth and a major second, about 17 per cent of the intervals being fourths and 60 per cent being major seconds. As these intervals do not characterize the entire material analyzed by the writer, it is interesting to find them in both groups of songs used in treating the sick. The interval of a fourth, as frequently stated, has been found to characterize songs concerning motion, and the major second is usually a passing tone. In these two songs it occurs most commonly as an ascending followed by a descending progression.

A rhythmic unit occurs in all the songs recorded by this singer and was present in all but one of the songs recorded by Pa′gitš. In the first three of the present group (Nos. 61–63) the rhythmic unit is characterized by a count-division of two eighth notes, this being the only count-division in the unit of No. 61. In Nos. 64 and 65 we find a unit comprising two quarter notes followed by a half note, but in No. 65 there is a second unit having a slightly different count-division.   No. 66, however, returns to the even eighth note division, the unit being twice as long as in No. 61 but otherwise the same. This peculiarity gives a rhythmic unity to the entire group.

The sequence of keys, which gave a certain melodic unity to the songs recorded by Pa′gitš, does not appear in this group, the keys of which are in the following order: D flat major, B flat minor, C major (two songs), and B flat major (two songs).   A peculiarity of Nos. 61, 64, and 65 is that the singer changed from a moderate to a fortissimo voice after singing the first few measures.   This peculiarity has not previously been noted by the writer.

PLOTS OF SONGS USED IN TREATMENT OF THE SICK

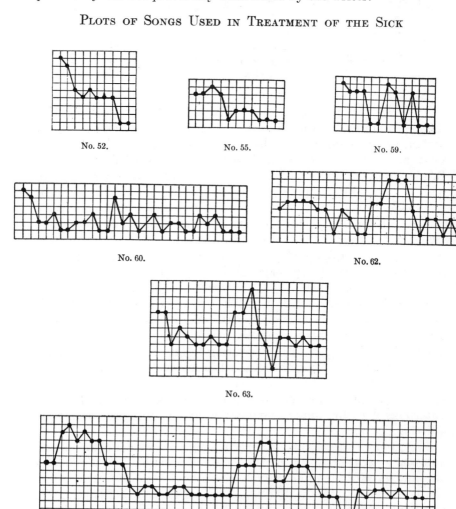

No. 52.

No. 55.

No. 59.

No. 60.

No. 62.

No. 63.

No. 64.

FIG. 12.—Plots, Group 10 (Treatment of sick)

The plots of this class of songs among the Ute do not show the emphasis on the lowest tone which prevailed in similar songs among the Sioux. (See Bull. 61, p. 283.)

Considering first the songs recorded by Pa'gitš (singer No. 11), we find Nos. 52–55 to be singularly uniform in type, characterized by a downward trend, with only one or two ascending progressions. This uniformity suggests steadiness and control.   In Nos. 59 and 60 the outline changes to larger progressions and an evident emphasis on the lowest tone.   It will be recalled that Nos. 59 and 60 were sung after the sick person had been somewhat restored by the action of the medicine man.

Throughout the plots of the songs recorded by Mrs. Washington (singer No. 25) there appears a resemblance, but the outlines themselves are not of a decided type.   The range is much wider than in the songs recorded by Pa'gitš and the lowest tone is used more frequently as an accented tone.   Four of her songs (two-thirds of the number) begin with an ascending progression.

SONGS USED IN TREATMENT OF SICK

MELODIC ANALYSIS

TABLE 1D.—TONALITY

	Number of songs	Serial Nos. of songs
Major tonality	10	52, 54, 58, 59, 60, 61, 63, 64, 65, 66.
Minor tonality	1	62.
Third lacking	4	53, 55, 56, 57.
Total	15	

TABLE 2D.—FIRST NOTE OF SONG—ITS RELATION TO KEYNOTE

	Number of songs	Serial Nos. of songs
Beginning on the—		
Octave	1	66.
Sixth	1	60.
Fifth	8	52, 53, 54, 59, 61, 63, 64, 65.
Fourth	1	62.
Second	1	58.
Keynote	3	55, 56, 57.
Total	15	

Songs Used in Treatment of Sick—Continued

MELODIC ANALYSIS—continued

TABLD 3D.—LAST NOTE OF SONG—ITS RELATION TO KEYNOTE

	Number of songs	Serial Nos. of songs
Ending on the—		
Fifth	7	52, 53, 55, 56, 57, 58, 59.
Keynote	8	54, 60, 61, 62, 63, 64, 65, 66.
Total	15	

TABLE 4D.—LAST NOTE OF SONG—ITS RELATION TO COMPASS OF SONG

	Number of songs	Serial Nos. of songs
Songs in which final t one is lowest tone in song	12	52, 53, 54, 55, 56, 57, 58, 59, 60, 62, 65, 66.
Songs containing a fourth below the final tone	3	61, 63, 64.
Total	15	

TABLE 5D.—NUMBER OF TONES COMPRISING COMPASS OF SONG

	Number of songs	Serial Nos. of songs
Compass of—		
Ten tones	2	64, 65.
Nine tones	1	52.
Eight tones	5	53, 61, 62, 63, 66.
Six tones	5	55, 57, 58, 59, 60.
Five tones	2	54, 56.
Total	15	

TABLE 6D.—TONE MATERIAL

	Number of songs	Serial Nos. of songs
Fourth five-toned scale	3	52, 59, 60.
Major triad and second	6	54, 58, 61, 64, 65, 66.
Minor triad and fourth	1	62.
Octave complete except seventh and sixth	1	63.
First, second, and fifth tones	1	53.
First, second, fifth, and sixth tones	3	55, 56, 57.
Total	15	

TABLE 7D.—ACCIDENTALS

	Number of songs	Serial Nos. of songs
Songs containing no accidentals	15	

Songs Used in Treatment of Sick—Continued

MELODIC ANALYSIS—continued

TABLE 8D.—STRUCTURE

	Number of songs	Serial Nos. of songs
Melodic	11	52, 53, 54, 55, 56, 57, 58, 59, 60, 62, 65.
Melodic with harmonic framework	4	61, 63, 64, 66.
Total	15	

TABLE 9D.—FIRST PROGRESSION—DOWNWARD AND UPWARD

	Number of songs	Serial Nos. of songs
Downward	5	53, 54, 60, 63, 66.
Upward	10	52, 55, 56, 57, 58, 59, 61, 62, 64, 65.
Total	15	

TABLE 10D.—TOTAL NUMBER OF PROGRESSIONS—DOWNWARD AND UPWARD

	Number of songs.	Serial Nos. of songs.
Downward	209	
Upward	151	
Total	360	

TABLE 11D.—INTERVALS IN DOWNWARD PROGRESSION

	Number of songs	Serial No. of songs
Interval of a--		
Minor sixth	2	
Fifth	1	
Fourth	40	
Major third	9	
Minor third	29	
Major second	127	
Minor second	1	
Total	209	

SONGS USED IN TREATMENT OF SICK—Continued

MELODIC ANALYSIS—continued

TABLE 12D.—INTERVALS IN UPWARD PROGRESSION

	Number of songs	Serial Nos. of songs
Interval of a—		
Major sixth	2	
Minor sixth	3	
Fifth	9	
Fourth	22	
Major third	9	
Minor third	13	
Major second	92	
Minor second	1	
Total	151	

TABLE 13D.—AVERAGE NUMBER OF SEMITONES IN AN INTERVAL

Total number of intervals.. 360
Total number of semitones... 1,076
Average number of semitones in an interval....................................... 2.9

TABLE 14D.—KEY

	Number of songs	Serial Nos. of songs
Key of—		
B flat major	2	65, 66.
B flat minor	1	62.
C major	2	63, 64.
D flat major	1	61.
E flat major	2	52, 54.
G major	3	58, 59, 60.
Irregular	4	52, 55, 56, 57.
Total	15	

RHYTHMIC ANALYSIS

TABLE 15D.—PART OF MEASURE ON WHICH SONG BEGINS

	Number of songs	Serial Nos. of songs
Beginning on unaccented part of measure	3	52, 54, 59.
Beginning on accented part of measure	12	53, 55, 56, 57, 58, 60, 61, 62, 63, 64, 65, 66.
Total	15	

Songs Used in Treatment of Sick—Continued

RHYTHMIC ANALYSIS—continued

TABLE 16D.—RHYTHM (METER) OF FIRST MEASURE

	Number of songs	Serial Nos. of songs
First measure in—		
2–4 time	12	52, 54, 55, 56, 58, 59, 60, 61, 62, 64, 65, 66.
3–4 time	3	52, 53, 57.
Total	15	

TABLE 17D.—CHANGE OF TIME, MEASURE-LENGTHS

	Number of songs	Serial Nos. of songs
Songs containing a change of time	15	

TABLE 18D.—RHYTHM (METER) OF DRUM

	Number of songs	Serial Nos. of songs
Drum not recorded	15	

TABLE 19D.—RHYTHMIC UNIT OF SONG

	Number of songs	Serial Nos. of songs
Songs containing—		
No rhythmic unit	1	53.
A rhythmic unit	12	52, 54, 55, 56, 57, 58, 59, 60, 61, 63, 64, 66.
Two rhythmic units	2	62, 65.
Total	15	

TABLE 20D.—TIME UNIT OF VOICE

	Number of songs	Serial Nos. of songs
Metronome—		
58	9	52, 53, 55, 57, 58, 59, 60, 62, 63.
63	1	60.
66	1	66.
76	2	54, 56.
88	1	65.
92	1	64.
Total	15	

Songs Used in Treatment of Sick—Continued

RHYTHMIC ANALYSIS—continued

TABLE 21D.—TIME UNIT OF DRUM

	Number of songs	Serial Nos. of songs
Drum not recorded	15	

TABLE 22D.—COMPARISON OF TIME UNIT OF VOICE AND DRUM

	Number of songs	Serial Nos. of songs
Drum not recorded	15	

WAR SONGS

While the general customs of war do not differ materially among Indian tribes, there are distinctive points in the customs of the several tribes that are of interest. Among the Utes, for instance, is noted the "washing of the wounded," and also a dancing in two circles, one within the other, when the scalps are carried in victory.

Several aged warriors of the Ute recorded war songs, but recalled them with difficulty, as the Utes have not been at war with another tribe for many years. Their former enemies were said to have been the Sioux and Arapaho, one purpose in war being the capture of horses from these tribes.

CHARACTERISTICS OF SONGS

A majority of the Sioux and Chippewa war songs were found to be minor in tonality, but 69 per cent of the Ute war songs are major in tonality. Firmness and directness are further shown by the ending of the same percentage on the keynote and the beginning of 56 per cent on the octave. Eighty-seven per cent begin with a downward progression. The melodic material is scanty, only about one-half the songs containing more than four degrees of the scale. The harmonic feeling is slight, only about 12 per cent being harmonic in structure. The average interval is slightly smaller than in the Bear dance, yet the percentage of intervals larger than a major third is higher in the war songs than in the Bear dance, this percentage being 22 in the Bear dance and 25 in the war songs. This is due to the more frequent occurrence of the interval of a fifth in the war songs. The accompanying instrument was a hand drum.

With three exceptions these songs begin on the unaccented portion of the measure, this being in contrast to the directness of beginning on the octave and ending on the keynote. There is a preference for 2–4 time, and only one song contains no change of measure-lengths. The rhythmic character of the songs is evident, as, with one exception, the songs contain one or more rhythmic units.

Black Otter (To'pātšuk, pl. 11, *a*) said that in the old days a man who wished to lead a war party requested that the people of his band be assembled at a certain place. When a camp had been established, the men who had been on previous war expeditions went to the chief's lodge and the chief announced the proposed undertaking. The men smoked and the chief explained the matter in detail. When Black Otter went to war the men rode on horses and used bows and arrows. He said the Utes formerly used stone arrow points, but that the men of his time had iron arrow points, the metal being obtained from the Mexicans and "shaped by rubbing with stone." The Indians made drinking cups from the knots of trees and carried these cups with them on the warpath. The night before a war party left the village a dance was held, and the warriors paraded through the camp in their war paraphernalia.

The following song was sung at the dance preceding the departure of a war party. In recording it Black Otter's voice trembled. He was almost overcome by emotion, saying it brought so strongly to his mind the friends and associates of former years.

No. 67. War Song (a)   (Catalogue No. 759)

Recorded by SINGER No. 1

VOICE ♩ = 126
DRUM ♩ = 126
Drum-rhythm similar to No. 20

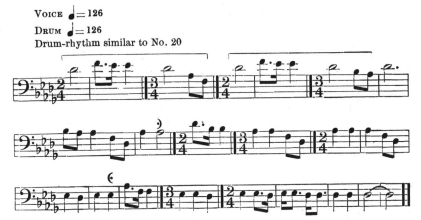

Analysis.—This song is on the fourth five-toned scale with D flat as its keynote. In structure it is melodic with harmonic framework. The rhythmic unit comprises three measures. Attention is directed to the ninth, tenth, and eleventh measures, which bear a close resemblance to the rhythmic unit, but were sung with a different accent and phrasing. The half note in the ninth measure was sung as the close of the preceding phrase, the tenth measure was begun with an accent, and the eleventh measure given two quarter notes instead of one half note. This distinction was clearly given in all renditions of the song.

The singer stated that the following song was sung by a war party when leaving the camp:

No. 68. War Song (b)   (Catalogue No. 704)

Recorded by Singer No. 9

Analysis.—This melody is simple in form, has a compass of an octave, and contains the tones of the fourth five-toned scale. It begins on the octave, and ends on the tonic, about two-thirds of the progressions being downward. In structure it is melodic. No rhythmic unit occurs and the song as a whole has not a decided rhythm. For other songs containing rests see No. 8.

No. 69. War Song (c)   (Catalogue No. 723)

Recorded by Singer No. 16

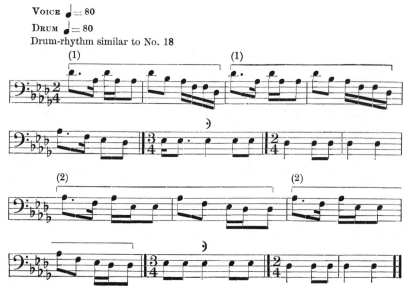

Analysis.—Several renditions of this song were recorded and show no material variation.   This is interesting to note, as the two rhythmic units differ only in the division of the final count.   The song is on the fourth five-toned scale and has a compass of an octave.   The fourth is a prominent interval, comprising more than a fourth of the entire number of progressions.   The association of this interval with songs concerning motion has been frequently noted.   This song resembles the song next following so closely as to suggest an unintentional duplication.

No. 70. War Song (d)   (Catalogue No. 792)

Recorded by SINGER No. 19

VOICE ♩ = 88
DRUM ♩ = 80
Drum-rhythm similar to No. 18

Analysis.—Between the renditions of this song there was sung a brief connective phrase which is represented in the transcription by two half notes, but which was sung with various divisions of the count.   It is of interest as showing the manner in which the Utes frequently break the ascent of an octave in repeating a song.   This is contrasted with the customs of the Sioux and Chippewa, who frequently make the direct ascent of an octave or a twelfth in repeating a song.   Songs having a connective phrase are noted in the analysis of No. 7.   This song is divided rhythmically into two parts, which are alike except for the fifth measure.   It will be readily noted that no measure corresponding to this appears after the rhythmic units in the second portion of the song.   Another slight difference is that the first part ends in 3–4 and the second in 2–4 time.   The tempo of the drum was not strictly maintained, but was slightly slower than the voice throughout the renditions.   The melody is on the fourth five-toned scale, and about three-fourths of the intervals are descending progressions.

One or more scouts, according to the size of the war party, were deployed to watch for the enemy. The following is a scout song and was said to have been sung by those who had been appointed to travel along a ridge of high land, probably parallel with the course taken by the war party. The scouts slept there, and as the sun rose they looked around but saw no trace of the enemy. The words are not transcribed, but were said to mean (freely translated) "There is no one near."

No. 71. Scout Song   (Catalogue No. 724)

Recorded by SINGER No. 16

Analysis.—This song contains only the tones of the minor triad and seventh, a tone-material which is considered in the analysis of No. 38. Throughout the rendition of this song the tone was firm and the intonation good. The descent of a seventh in two intervals, occurring in the rhythmic unit, is effective and is barbaric in character. The intervals are large, and only 19 progressions occur in the song. The tempo is quite slow. The interval of a fifth is prominent in this song, 42 per cent of the progressions being fifths.

The following song was said to be that of a scout who perceived that the enemy was near. The song was sometimes used as a parade song. The singer, a comparatively young man, said that he learned the song from the old men when he was a boy.

No. 72. War Song (e)   (Catalogue No. 705)

Recorded by SINGER No. 9

Analysis.—Instead of a uniform drumbeat throughout the song, we have in this instance a very rapid drumbeat in the opening measures, followed by a quarter-note rhythm. Other songs with the same peculiarity are Nos. 86, 87, and 88. This seems an individual phase rather than one connected with the character of the song. The quarter-note drumbeat was maintained steadily during the 3-8 measures of the song and synchronized occasionally with the voice. Only one other song (No. 22) begins in 3-8 time. In the fourth and fifth renditions the singer interpolated sharp, shrill cries before the connective phrase. (See No. 7.) The melody contains the tones of the fourth five-toned scale and is melodic in structure. Only one-fourth of the intervals are larger than a minor third.

One of the oldest warriors in the tribe said that his father told him of a war party in which he was leader. It was a large party, comprising from 30 to 50 men, armed with bows and arrows. The information is not clear as to whether this song was sung by the attacking warriors when near the enemy's camp or was composed in honor of a successful attack. To sing during an attack is not customary, yet it may have been done at this time, as the attacking party was so large. The singer's manner was excited as he recorded the song, and between the renditions he shouted, "Now, now, run your horses because our young men may be killed; because if we go into the enemy's tents our scalps may be taken." The attack was said to have been made just before sunrise.

No. 73. War Song (f)   (Catalogue No. 747)

Recorded by SINGER No. 18

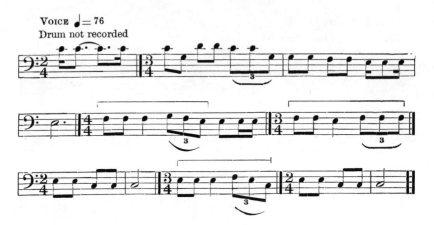

Analysis.—Two renditions of this song were recorded with practically no variations. In both renditions the second count in the second measure was sung as two eighth notes, thus differentiating it from the rhythmic unit in which the corresponding count is sung as a quarter note. Neither are the divisions of the last count like those in the following measure. Only about one-eighth of the intervals are larger than a major third, and more than half are major and minor seconds. (See No. 28.) The song has a compass of an octave.

The scalps secured by a war party were not fastened in a hoop but tied at the end of a pole "higher than a man's head." It was customary for returning warriors to give a scalp to a woman whose husband or son had been killed in war, also to a man who had lost a near relative on the warpath. A returned war party paraded around the camp at about 8 o'clock in the morning. In this parade the scalps were carried on poles or fastened to the chin straps of the horses. Some of the men had women behind them on their horses. All were in gala attire and the leaders accompanied the songs by pounding on hand drums. The following song was used on such an occasion:

No. 74. Parade of returning warriors   (Catalogue No. 748)

Recorded by SINGER No. 18

VOICE ♩ = 66
DRUM ♩ = 66
Drum-rhythm similar to No. 20

Analysis.—This song is on the fourth five-toned scale with G flat as its keynote. Two renditions were recorded, each containing a repeated portion as indicated in the transcription. Two rhythmic units occur, the difference between them being slight but clearly given by the singer. The song is melodic in structure, and almost half the intervals are major seconds.

No. 75. War Song (g)   (Catalogue No. 749)

Recorded by SINGER No. 18

VOICE ♩ = 63

DRUM ♩ = 63

Drum-rhythm similar to No. 20

Analysis.—This song is characterized by a compass of 12 tones, which is unusual in this series. The song contains no change of time, differing in this respect from a majority of the present songs. The rhythmic unit is interesting and occurs seven times. Ascending and descending intervals are almost equal in number, the song containing 10 ascending and 10 descending major thirds. The melody contains only the tones of the major triad.

A peculiar custom noted among the Utes was that of "washing the wounded." This was done at the scalp dances, the body of a wounded warrior being placed in the center of the dancing circle and his wounds washed as certain songs were sung. The same was done if a man had been killed and his body brought home by the war party. Two songs of this act were recorded, and it was said the same songs were used for any occasion of mourning and also, strangely, were used on occasions of rejoicing.

No. 76. Song when washing the wounded (a)

(Catalogue No. 725)

Recorded by SINGER No. 16

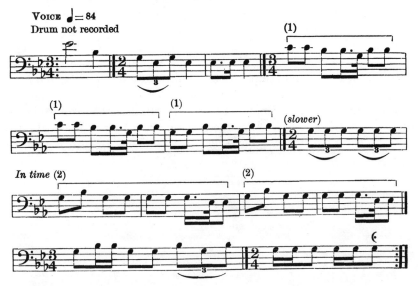

Analysis.—A peculiarity of this song is the measure in slower time, this change in tempo being the same in all renditions. (See No. 11.) The phrasing was clearly given throughout the song. Sixty per cent of the intervals are minor thirds, about equally divided between ascending and descending progressions. The song contains only the tones of the major triad and sixth.

No. 77. Song when washing the wounded (b)

(Catalogue No. 706)

Recorded by SINGER No. 9

VOICE ♩ = 104
Drum not recorded

Analysis.—This song was recorded by the same singer at two different times, thus affording an interesting opportunity for observing the accuracy with which the song was repeated. (Cf. Nos. 39 and

78.) Six renditions were recorded in 1914, the renditions being uniform and connected without a break in the time. The transcription is from the cylinder made in 1914. Five renditions of the same song were recorded in 1916, at which time the writer did not play the first record, but "hummed" the transcription. The singer recognized it and said he would like to make another record of it. This second cylinder was transcribed and the results compared. In this comparison it is found that all the renditions recorded in 1916 omit the fifth and sixth measures and the last measure of the song as transcribed. As these measures are repetitions, this would be of slight importance, but as it reduces the occurrences of these phrases from three to two the change suggests a tendency toward regularity

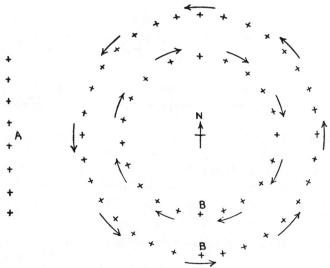

Fig. 13.—Diagram, Scalp dance.   a, Singers with hand drums.   b, Two circles of women moving in opposite directions.

and conventionality. The first group of renditions was in a tempo of $\downarrow = 104$, and the key of G minor; the second was faster ($\downarrow = 108$) but in a lower key—the key of F sharp minor. The 5–4 division of certain measures was strictly maintained. The song contains the tones of the second five-toned scale and is melodic in structure. Considering the lack of variety in progressions the melody is interesting and quite diversified. One-half the intervals are minor thirds, and of the other half all except one interval are major seconds, that interval being an ascending fourth. Other songs containing rests are noted in the analysis of No. 8.

The dancing with the scalps (commonly known as the Scalp dance) began late in the afternoon and ended soon after dark. There was no feast connected with this dance. The singers stood in a line facing the east, the men with hand drums being in the center of the line. In front of the men were two circles of women dancers, one circle being inside the other.   The two circles moved in opposite directions, the inner one moving "with the sun."   Each group of women had a leader, who wore a feather war bonnet.   The leader of the inner circle was the wife of the chief, and only she was allowed to carry a scalp on a pole.   The arrangement of the dancers is shown in the accompanying diagram (fig. 13).

At the conclusion of the Scalp dances it was customary to take the scalps to the chief.   He had a large tipi with tall poles, and the scalps were fastened at the tops of these poles, where they remained undisturbed.

No. 78. Scalp Dance Song (a)   (Catalogue No. 760)

Recorded by SINGER No. 1

VOICE ♩ = 96
Drum not recorded

Analysis.—This song was twice recorded by the same singer, only one of the records being transcribed (cf. Nos. 39 and 77).   The repetition arose from an impression frequently noted among the Indians, that if the words are changed in a melody it becomes a different song.   Thus, in the first instance, the singer said this was a song which he sang in the war dance when he brought home a captive woman, and, in the second instance, he said it was a scalp dance song.   The words were not taken in either rendition.

A comparison of the two cylinders shows the pitch of the renditions to be the same.   Five repetitions of the song were recorded the first time and six the second time.   The differences in these 11 renditions are too slight to be of importance.   In the first group the opening phrase was occasionally repeated, and in the second group the ending was occasionally changed in rhythm, and the fifth measure (last two counts) contained quarter in place of eighth notes.   Passing from this comparison to an analysis of the transcription, we note that the melody contains only the tones of the minor triad and fourth and in structure is melodic with harmonic framework.   More than half the intervals are minor thirds, a majority of the remainder being major seconds.

No. 79. Scalp Dance Song (b)   (Catalogue No. 750)

Recorded by SINGER No. 18

VOICE ♩= 66

DRUM ♩= 66
Drum-rhythm similar to No. 20

Analysis.—Considering F to be the keynote of this song, we find the tone material to comprise the keynote, third, and fourth. The structure of the song shows, however, what has been termed an "interval-formation" rather than a key-relation of the several tones. (See Bull. 53, pp. 7, 8.) Thus the first portion, and in every instance the rhythmic unit, is on the fifth (B flat–F), while the middle and closing measures are on the minor third (F–A flat). The intervals are larger than in a majority of these songs, about one-fourth of them being fifths. The major second comprises only about one-sixth of the total number. Drum and voice have the same time unit, but because of slight variations in tempo they seldom coincide for more than a few measures.

No. 80. Scalp Dance Song (c)   (Catalogue No. 751)

Recorded by SINGER No. 18

VOICE ♪ = 169
Drum not recorded

Analysis.—The measure-divisions in this song were clearly given in all the renditions, and as the tempo is so rapid it is considered

advisable that the time unit be indicated as an eighth note. The rhythmic unit occurs twice and is peculiar in character. The fourth is a prominent interval, comprising more than one-fourth of the progressions. The minor third appears with about the same frequency. In structure the song is melodic with harmonic framework, and the melody tones are those of the major triad and sixth.

No. 81. War Song (h)   (Catalogue No. 794)

Recorded by SINGER No. 20 (Charles Mack, pl. 11, *c*)

Analysis.—This song has a compass of 11 tones and is on the second five-toned scale. One rhythmic unit occurs which is long and varied in count-divisions. The several renditions of the song show no material variation. In structure the song is melodic. Twenty-five of the 33 progressions are minor thirds and major seconds. Of the remainder all but one are fourths.

No. 82. War Song (i)   (Catalogue No. 795)

Recorded by SINGER No. 20

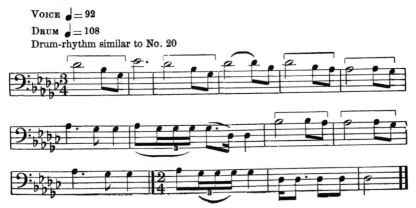

Analysis.—This song, like many others of the present series, progresses chiefly by whole tones (see No. 28), yet it is a melody with abundant variety and interest. In structure it is melodic and contains the tones of the major triad and second. The drum is slightly faster than the voice and its tempo was steadily maintained. A rhythmic unit occurs six times in the song.

PLOTS OF WAR SONGS

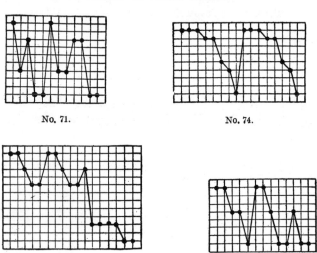

No. 71.   No. 74.

No. 75.   No. 79.

FIG. 14.—Plots, Group 11 (War songs)

While a few of the war songs show the ordinary type of steadily descending trend broken by one or two ascending progressions, we find that about one-half of them contain a wideness of interval which has not been noted in any group of songs previously plotted.

WAR SONGS

MELODIC ANALYSIS

TABLE 1E.—TONALITY

	Number of songs	Serial Nos. of songs
Major tonality	11	67, 68, 69, 70, 72, 73, 74, 75, 76, 80, 82.
Minor tonality	5	71, 77, 78, 79, 81.
Total	16	

WAR SONGS—Continued

MELODIC ANALYSIS—continued

TABLE 2E.—FIRST NOTE OF SONG—ITS RELATION TO KEYNOTE

	Number of songs	Serial Nos. of songs
Beginning on the—		
Twelfth	1	75.
Octave	9	67, 68, 69, 70, 73, 76, 78, 79, 80.
Sixth	1	74.
Fifth	4	71, 72, 77, 82.
Fourth	1	81.
Total	16	

TABLE 3E.—LAST NOTE OF SONG—ITS RELATION TO KEYNOTE

	Number of songs	Serial Nos. of songs
Ending on the—		
Fifth	3	71, 74, 82.
Third	2	76, 80.
Keynote	11	67, 68, 69, 70, 72, 73, 75, 77, 78, 79, 81.
Total	16	

TABLE 4E.—LAST NOTE OF SONG—ITS RELATION TO COMPASS OF SONG

	Number of songs	Serial Nos. of songs
Songs in which final tone is—		
Lowest tone in song	12	67, 68, 69, 70, 71, 72, 73, 75, 77, 78, 79, 81.
Immediately preceded by—		
Major third below	2	76, 80.
Whole tone below with fourth below in a previous measure	1	77.
Songs containing a fourth below the final tone	1	72.
Total	16	

TABLE 5E.—NUMBER OF TONES COMPRISING COMPASS OF SONG

	Number of songs	Serial Nos. of songs
Compass of—		
Twelve tones	1	75.
Eleven tones	1	81.
Ten tones	2	67, 71.
Nine tones	4	72, 74, 80, 82.
Eight tones	8	68, 69, 70, 73, 76, 77, 78, 79.
Total	16	

WAR SONGS—Continued

MELODIC ANALYSIS—continued

TABLE 6E.—TONE MATERIAL

	Number of songs	Serial Nos. of songs
Second five-toned scale	2	77, 81.
Fourth five-toned scale	6	67, 68, 69, 70, 72, 74.
Major triad	1	75.
Major triad and sixth	2	76, 80.
Major triad and second	1	82.
Minor triad and seventh	1	71.
Minor triad and fourth	1	78.
Octave complete except seventh and sixth	1	73.
Minor third and fourth	1	79.
Total	16	

TABLE 7E.—ACCIDENTALS

	Number of songs	Serial Nos. of songs
Songs containing—		
No accidentals	15	67, 68, 69, 70, 71, 73, 74, 75, 76, 77, 78, 79, 80, 81, 82.
Fourth raised a semitone	1	72.
Total	16	

TABLE 8E.—STRUCTURE

	Number of songs	Serial Nos. of songs
Melodic	8	68, 70, 71, 72, 74, 77, 81, 82.
Melodic with harmonic framework	6	67, 69, 73, 76, 78, 80.
Harmonic	2	75, 79.
Total	16	

TABLE 9E.—FIRST PROGRESSION—DOWNWARD AND UPWARD

	Number of songs	Serial Nos. of songs
Downward	14	68, 69, 70, 72, 73, 74, 75, 76, 77, 78, 79, 80, 81, 82.
Upward	2	67, 71.
Total	16	

WAR SONGS—Continued

MELODIC ANALYSIS—continued

TABLE 10E.—TOTAL NUMBER OF PROGRESSIONS—DOWNWARD AND UPWARD

	Number of songs	Serial Nos. of songs
Downward	285	
Upward	175	
Total	460	

TABLE 11E.—INTERVALS IN DOWNWARD PROGRESSION

	Number of songs	Serial Nos. of songs
Interval of a—		
Minor sixth	1	
Fifth	16	
Fourth	38	
Major third	31	
Minor third	83	
Major second	110	
Minor second	6	
Total	285	

TABLE 12E.—INTERVALS IN UPWARD PROGRESSION

	Number of songs	Serial Nos. of songs
Interval of a—		
Ninth	1	
Octave	3	
Seventh	1	
Major sixth	3	
Minor sixth	4	
Fifth	26	
Fourth	24	
Major third	10	
Minor third	52	
Major second	46	
Minor second	5	
Total	175	

TABLE 13E.—AVERAGE NUMBER OF SEMITONES IN AN INTERVAL

Total number of intervals	460
Total number of semitones	1,625
Average number of semitones in an interval	3,5

WAR SONGS—Continued

MELODIC ANALYSIS—continued

TABLE 14E.—KEY

	Number of songs	Serial Nos. of songs
Key of—		
B flat minor	1	81.
B major	1	75.
C major	1	73.
D flat major	3	67, 69, 70.
D major	1	68.
E flat major	2	76, 80.
E flat minor	1	78.
F minor	1	79.
G flat major	2	74, 82.
A flat major	1	72.
G sharp minor	2	71, 77.
Total	16	

RHYTHMIC ANALYSIS

TABLE 15E.—PART OF MEASURE ON WHICH SONG BEGINS

	Number of songs	Serial Nos. of songs
Beginning on unaccented part of measure	13	67, 68, 69, 70, 72, 73, 74, 76,77, 78, 79, 80, 82.
Beginning on accented part of measure	3	71, 75, 81.
Total	16	

TABLE 16E.—RHYTHM (METER) OF FIRST MEASURE

	Number of songs	Serial Nos. of songs
First measure in—		
2–4 time	9	67, 69, 70, 71, 73, 74, 75, 77, 79.
3–4 time	5	68, 76, 78, 81, 82.
3–8 time	1	72.
4–8 time	1	80.
Total	16	

TABLE 17E.—CHANGE OF TIME, MEASURE LENGTHS

	Number of songs	Serial Nos. of songs
Songs containing no change of time	1	75.
Songs containing a change of time	15	67, 68, 69, 70, 71, 72, 73, 74, 76, 77, 78, 79, 80, 81, 82.
Total	16	

War Songs—Continued

RHYTHMIC ANALYSIS—continued

TABLE 18E.—RHYTHM (METER) OF DRUM

	Number of songs	Serial Nos. of songs
Eighth notes unaccented	3	69, 70, 81.
Quarter notes unaccented	5	67, 74, 75, 79, 82.
Rapid beat resembling a tremolo at opening of song, followed by a quarter-note beat	1	72.
Drum not recorded	7	68, 71, 73, 76, 77, 78, 80.
Total	16	

TABLE 19E.—RHYTHMIC UNIT OF SONG

	Number of songs	Serial Nos. of songs
Songs containing—		
No rhythmic unit	1	68.
One rhythmic unit	11	67, 70, 71, 72, 73, 75, 77, 78, 79, 80, 82.
Two rhythmic units	4	69, 74, 76, 81.
Total	16	

TABLE 20E.—TIME UNIT OF VOICE

	Number of songs	Serial Nos. of songs
Metronome—		
60	1	81.
63	1	75.
66	3	74, 78, 79.
69	1	71.
76	1	73.
80	1	69.
84	2	68, 76.
88	1	70.
92	1	82.
104	1	77.
126	2	67, 72.
168	1	80.
Total	16	

WAR SONGS—Continued

RHYTHMIC ANALYSIS—continued

TABLE 21E.—TIME UNIT OF DRUM [1]

	Number of songs	Serial Nos. of songs
Metronome—		
60	1	81.
63	2	72, 75.
66	2	74, 79.
80	1	69.
88	1	70.
108	1	82.
126	1	67.
Drum not recorded	7	68, 71, 73, 76, 77, 78, 80.
Total	16	

TABLE 22E.—COMPARISON OF TIME UNIT OF VOICE AND DRUM

	Number of songs	Serial Nos. of songs
Time unit of voice and drum the same	7	67, 69, 72, 74, 75, 79, 81.
Voice faster than drum	1	70.
Voice slower than drum	1	82.
Drum not recorded	7	68, 71, 73, 76, 77, 78, 80.
Total	16	

[1] A tremolo drumbeat precedes the even beat in No. 72.

PARADE SONGS

In former times if the Utes were gathered in a large camp a "parade" took place every morning. Such a parade was noted in the description of the Sun dance (p. 80). Both men and women were on horseback, the men preceding the women. At the head of the procession rode two leaders side by side, beating on hand drums, while all the company sang the Parade songs. These songs were numerous and popular.

CHARACTERISTICS OF SONGS

The principal characteristic of Parade songs is an ornamentation comprising small note values. Examples of this occur in Nos. 84, 87, 89, 90, and 93. These did not vary in the repetitions of the song. About half the songs contain no rhythmic unit, showing the rhythmic feeling to be less than the melodic. With one exception the Parade songs are major in tonality. The compass is unusually large, all the songs having a range of an octave or more than an octave. Only one song is harmonic in structure, and a majority begin with a downward progression.

No. 83. Parade Song (a)   (Catalogue No. 696)

Recorded by SINGER No. 4

VOICE ♩— 63
Drum not recorded

Analysis.—The slow tempo of this song was steadily maintained throughout three renditions, which were sung without a break in the time. The melody progresses chiefly by whole tones, which constitute two-thirds of the intervals. The song is melodic in structure and contains all the tones of the octave except the seventh.

No. 84. Parade Song (b)   (Catalogue No. 707)

Recorded by SINGER No. 9

VOICE ♩= 66
DRUM ♩= 66
Drum-rhythm similar to No 20

Analysis.—The rendering of this song was particularly clear in intonation and count divisions, not varying in the repetitions. Drum and voice have the same time unit and are synchronous. The song is peculiar in that the only progressions are fifths, fourths, and semitones, and also in that the ascending and descending progressions are almost equal in number. The melody tones are those of the major triad and second, and the structure of the song is melodic with harmonic framework. (Concerning the connective phrase see No. 7.)

No. 85. Parade Song (c)   (Catalogue No. 708)

Recorded by SINGER No. 9

VOICE ♩= 92
Drum not recorded

Analysis.—Five renditions of this song were recorded, two being separated by shrill cries and the others connected by a short phrase. (See No. 7.) In every rendition the accent is changed in the last occurrence of the rhythmic unit. Minor thirds and major seconds are the principal intervals of progression, though the variety of intervals is greater than in a majority of the Ute songs under analysis.

No. 86. Parade Song (d)   (Catalogue No. 709)

Recorded by SINGER No. 9

VOICE ♩= 66
DRUM ♩= 66
Drum-rhythm similar to No. 72

Analysis.—This melody contains six kinds of intervals in ascending progression, which is an unusual number. The drumbeat in the first four measures of the first rendition was tremolo, after which the quarter-note beat was continuous. (See No. 72.) Drum and voice have the same time unit, determined by the majority of the measures, but the drum is steadily maintained, while the voice tempo varies slightly. The time of the transcription should be understood as indicating the accents and the approximate note values rather than actual durations of time, resembling some of the songs in which the pitch indicated by the notation is only approximate. These variabilities are too slight to be shown in any except an exceedingly detailed graphic form, the transcription showing, however, the trend of the melody with sufficient exactness for our present purpose. Four renditions were recorded and contain no important differences. The connective phrase in this song is unusually long. Another song using a similar phrase between renditions is No. 7.

No. 87. Parade Song (e)   (Catalogue No. 771)

Recorded by SINGER No. 17

VOICE ♩ = 63
DRUM ♩ = 63
Drum-rhythm similar to No. 72

Analysis.—Drum and voice have the same time unit in this song, but because of slight variations in tempo they never exactly coincide. In each rendition the drumbeat was tremolo to the point marked X, after which it was in quarter notes. (See No. 72.) Three rhythmic units occur, the first being emphatic in character and appearing always on the same tones, which is unusual. The third unit differs from the second only in the division of the last count, but this difference was steadily maintained. The tone material is that of the fourth five-toned scale and the song has a compass of 12 tones. The average interval in this song comprises four semitones. Reference to the tables of analysis on page 42 will show this to be an unusually large interval.

No. 88. Parade Song (f)   (Catalogue No. 762)

Recorded by SINGER No. 16

VOICE ♩ = 66

DRUM ♩ = 66

Drum-rhythm similar to No. 72

Analysis.—This song has a compass of 12 tones and contains the major triad and second. In structure it is melodic with harmonic framework. The drumbeat was tremolo to the point marked X, after which in four renditions it was in quarter-note values. (See No. 72.) The repetitions of the song necessitate an ascending interval of a twelfth, which was sung with good intonation. The fourth is the interval of most frequent occurrence, constituting 54 per cent of the entire number of intervals. (See No. 3.) This interval has frequently been noted as associated with the idea of motion.

No. 89. Parade Song (g)   (Catalogue No. 780)

Recorded by SINGER No. 21

VOICE ♩ = 60

DRUM ♩ = 60

Drum-rhythm similar to No. 20

Connective phrase

Analysis.—This song has a compass of 10 tones and contains all the tones of the octave. More than half the progressions are whole tones. (See No. 28.) The lowest tone in the third measure was not always sung clearly, the descent to this tone being glissando.   The time was steadily maintained throughout all the renditions, which were uniform in every respect.   Other songs using a connective phrase are noted in the analysis of No. 7.

No. 90. Parade Song (h)   (Catalogue No. 793)

Recorded by SINGER No. 19

VOICE ♩ = 80

DRUM ♩ = 80
Drum-rhythm similar to No. 18

Analysis.—The interval of a fourth comprises 52 per cent of the progressions in this song.   (See No. 3.)   No rhythmic unit occurs, and the song is not particularly rhythmic in structure.   The song is major in tonality, melodic in structure, and contains all the tones of the octave except the seventh.

No. 91. Parade Song (i)   (Catalogue No. 735)

Recorded by SINGER No. 7

VOICE ♩ = 132

DRUM ♩ = 132
Drum-rhythm similar to No. 20

Analysis.—Few songs of the present series are so typical as this, yet the quality which makes it typical is hard to define.   Two-thirds of the intervals are minor thirds and major seconds, but in this it resembles many other songs. Neither is the proportion of ascending and descending intervals unusual, there being 40 per cent of ascending and 60 per cent of descending progressions. But the song is minor in tonality with a special prominence of the subdominant. This is quite unusual and worthy of consideration by students. The melody tones are those of the second five-toned scale with the seventh sharped. The tonic chord appears as the framework of the melody. The ascent of an octave in the first measure and the beginning and ending on the same tone are noted in the analysis of No. 37. A short connective phrase was sung between the renditions. (See No. 7.)

No. 92. Parade Song (j)   (Catalogue No. 761)

Recorded by SINGER No. 1

Analysis.—Throughout the renditions of this song the intonation on the descending minor third was faulty, yet the fourth and octave were sung with good intonation. The fourth constitutes about one-third of the progressions. The song is harmonic in structure and contains the tones of the major triad and fourth. (Concerning the use of a connective phrase see No. 7.)

No. 93. Parade Song (k)   (Catalogue No. 762)

Recorded by SINGER No. 1

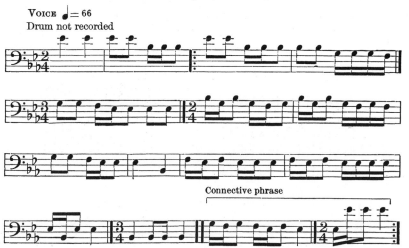

Analysis.—The rhythmic structure of this song is worthy of special attention. The first two measures were sung only once, after which the remainder of the song as transcribed was sung four times, the last rendition ending at the double bar. An introductory phrase is rarely used in Ute songs, though appearing frequently in the songs of the Chippewa. Other songs of this series containing a connective phrase are noted in the analysis of No. 7. In all the renditions of this song the count divisions were as indicated. The song comprises two rhythmic periods which resemble each other yet show enough difference to give variety and character to the song as a whole. The first period comprises the third, fourth, and fifth measures, and the second comprises the three following measures. A comparison of these will show the variations. The song has a compass of 11 tones and contains the major triad and second. The whole tone is the chief interval of progression (see No. 24). Although the song is major in tonality, the major third does not appear as a progression.

PLOTS OF PARADE SONGS

A wide compass and sharply descending trend characterize the plots of a majority of these songs. The Parade songs were sung on horseback, but with two exceptions (Nos. 86 and 92) the plots do not show the profile that has been associated with songs concerning

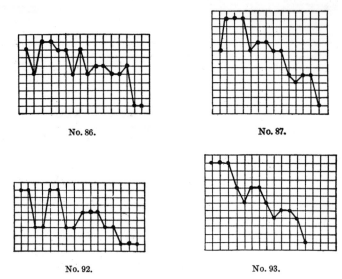

No. 86.   No. 87.

No. 92.   No. 93.

FIG. 15.—Plots, Group 12 (Parade songs)

animals. Even in No. 86 the rise and fall of the outline is not from the lowest tone, as has been noted in the plots of songs concerning animals in motion.

HAND GAME SONGS

Among the Ute, as among other tribes, this game is played extensively and large stakes are placed upon its success. The implements of the game used by the Uinta Ute at White Rocks, Utah, and collected by Culin in 1900 comprise "four slender, highly polished bones, 3½ inches in length; two bound with a strip of leather in the middle." [23] The game among the Yampa Ute in northwestern Colorado was observed in 1877 by Mr. Edwin A. Barber and described as follows: "A row of players, consisting of five or six or a dozen men, is arranged on either side of a tent, facing each other. Before each man is placed a bundle of small twigs or sticks, each 6 to 8 inches in length and pointed at one end. Every tête-à-tête couple is provided with two cylindrical bone dice, carefully fashioned and highly polished, which measure about 2 inches in length and half an inch

---

[23] Culin, Stewart, Games of the North American Indians, 24th Ann. Rept. Bur. Amer. Ethn., p. 315. Washington, 1907.

in diameter, one being white and the other black, or sometimes ornamented with a black band. * * * One of the gamblers incloses a die in each hand and, placing one above the other, allows the upper bone to pass into the other hand with the other die. This process is reversed again and again, while all the time the hands are shaken up and down in order to mystify the partner in the passing of the dice. The other man during the performance hugs himself tightly by crossing his arms and placing either hand under the opposite arm and, with a dancing motion of the body, swaying to and fro, watches the shuffling of the dice with the closest attention. When this has gone on for a few minutes, the latter suddenly points with one arm at the opposite arm of his partner and strikes himself under that arm with the other hand. Whichever hand of his rival he chooses is to be opened, and if the dice are in it the guesser takes them and proceeds in the same manner. If, however, he misses, and the dice are not there, he forfeits one counter, and this is taken from his bundle and stuck in the ground. Thus the game continues until one or the other has gained every stick." [24]

In the game as observed by Barber the hand game songs were accompanied by beating on "rude parchment-covered drums," but the writer was informed that on the Uinta and Ouray Reservation the songs were formerly accompanied by beating on a horizontal pole, the singers being seated on either side of the pole and each holding two sticks with which they beat in time to the song.

CHARACTERISTICS OF SONGS

Two peculiarities are found in these songs and in no others of the present series: (1) A sliding upward of the tone on ascending progressions, resembling the sliding downward which appeared in songs of the Bear dance; (2) a sharply accented tone followed by a short rest. Concerning the first-named peculiarity it is interesting to note that after this observation had been made by the writer a comment by Barber came to her attention, corroborating it by a statement written more than 40 years previously. The following notation (fig. 16), taken from Barber's article, indicates the sliding upward of the voice. Barber states, concerning the Ute hand game song: "No words are sung, but the syllable *ah* is pronounced in a whining, nasal tone for every note. * * * The war and dance songs of the Ute are different from this, yet they are somewhat similar." [25]

The sliding upward of the voice, as well as the second-named peculiarity of the hand game songs, appear in Nos. 94–99. Four-fifths of the songs are major in tonality, two-thirds are harmonic in

[24] Barber, Edwin A, Gaming among the Utah Indians. American Naturalist, vol. XI, no. 6, pp. 351–352. Boston, 1877.

[25] Ibid., pp. 352, 353.

structure, and 7 of the 10 songs contain a rhythmic unit. No interval larger than a fifth occurs in these songs, and about one-third of the intervals are whole tones. Thus it is seen the progressions are smaller than in many of the songs under analysis. This, together with the large proportion of songs having a rhythmic unit, shows that rhythm is a more important phase than melody in the hand game songs. The average interval is 3.2 semitones, with which we contrast the average interval in the Chippewa moccasin game songs, which was 3.5 semitones. Only 33 per cent of the moccasin game songs con-

FIG. 16.—Music of hand game song noted in 1877

tained a rhythmic unit. As the Ute hand game, with its beating on a pole as accompaniment, appears more primitive than the Chippewa moccasin game it is interesting to note the greater importance of rhythm in the Ute songs. No words were used with these songs.

No. 94. Hand Game Song (a)　　(Catalogue No. 697)

Recorded by SINGER No. 4

Analysis.—This song is characterized by a sliding upward of tone and by short rests. (See No. 8.) The rhythmic unit is interesting and occurs twice. Five renditions were given with no break in the time, the final measure always containing three counts, as transcribed. The song is harmonic in structure and the intervals are more varied than in a majority of these songs. The melody tones are those of the major triad and second.

No. 95. Hand Game Song (b)   (Catalogue No. 736)

Recorded by SINGER No. 7

VOICE ♩ = 120
DRUM ♩ = 120
Drum-rhythm similar to No. 18

Analysis.—This, like the preceding song, contains a sliding upward tone and also short rests. (See No. 8.) The rhythmic unit furnishes the chief interest of the song, occurring three times on the same tones. The song is harmonic in structure and has a compass of six tones. Although the compass is so small the interval of a fifth occurs twice.

No. 96. Hand Game Song (c)   (Catalogue No. 796)

Recorded by SINGER No. 22

VOICE ♩ = 100
DRUM ♩ = 100
Drum-rhythm similar to No. 18

Analysis.—Five renditions of this peculiar melody were recorded, the only differences being that in one rendition a certain phrase was repeated. As indicated, there was no break in the time between the renditions. The rhythmic unit gives coherence to the melody, and it is possible to show this in notation, though the peculiar manner of singing can not be graphically shown. The song contains 16 progressions, 13 of which are fourths. (See No. 3.) It has a compass of six tones and contains the tones of the major triad and second. For other songs containing rests see No. 8.

25043°—22——12

No. 97. Hand Game Song (d)   (Catalogue No. 745)

Recorded by SINGER No. 6

VOICE ♩ = 92
DRUM ♩ = 116
Drum-rhythm similar to No. 18

Analysis.—The time was not rigidly maintained in the renditions of this song, but the drum was persistently a little faster than the voice. The renditions differ very slightly, in some the second count of the first measure being omitted. It will be noted that this omission makes the two parts of the song alike. The progressions are 30 in number, 26 being minor thirds and 4 major thirds, yet G is the implied keynote of the melody. The song begins and ends on the same tone, which is unusual. (See No. 37.) Other songs containing rests are noted in the analysis of No. 8.

No. 98. Hand Game Song (e)   (Catalogue No. 737)

Recorded by SINGER No. 7

VOICE ♩ = 112
DRUM ♩ = 112
Drum-rhythm similar to No. 18

Analysis.—This is a very short melody, but is characteristic and strongly rhythmic. The only interval is the major second. (See No. 28.) The rest in the first measure was clearly defined. (See No. 8.) Seven renditions were recorded with no break in the time.

No. 99. Hand Game Song (f)   (Catalogue No. 698)

Recorded by SINGER No. 4.

Analysis.—The part of this song preceding the change of time was sung only once, followed by the second part, which was sung nine times without a break in the time. The first part is a pleasing melody with little character. The second part is unmistakably a hand game song, resembling No. 98. As the singer was considered a reliable informant, the song is presented as it was sung. It has a compass of nine tones and contains the tones of the fourth five-toned scale; 58 progressions occur, 40 of which are major seconds (whole tones). (Concerning the change of tempo see No. 11.)

No. 100. Hand Game Song (g)   (Catalogue No. 797)

Recorded by SINGER No 22

Drum-rhythm

Analysis.—Six renditions of this song were recorded and show no differences except that the second count of the third measure was occasionally sung as two eighth notes. The song presents some interesting points of rhythm. Thus we note that the last count of the second measure contains a reversal of the count divisions in the second count of the rhythmic unit. The fifth measure contains in its second count a division resembling that of the rhythmic unit but which was uniformly sung as two sixteenths instead of an eighth note. The only progressions are fourths and major seconds. In ascending progression there are seven fourths and three whole tones, and in descending progression there are eight fourths and three whole tones. Considering A to be the keynote of the melody, its tones are the keynote, fourth, and fifth. Four drumbeats were equivalent in time to one quarter note of the melody; the drum is therefore regarded as having a rhythm of sixteenth notes. Drum and voice were synchronous at the beginning of each count.

No. 101. Hand Game Song (h)   (Catalogue No. 738)

Recorded by SINGER No. 7

Analysis.—In all the four renditions of this song the division of the first count in the first measure was different from that of the corresponding count in the third measure.   These slight differences repeated persistently show that the rhythm of the song is clear in the mind of the singer.   This song is harmonic in structure and has a compass of five tones.   The major third constitutes 76 per cent of the progressions, the remaining intervals being four minor thirds and one ascending fifth.

No. 102. Hand Game Song (i)   (Catalogue No. 699)

Recorded by SINGER No. 4

VOICE ♩ = 104
DRUM ♩ = 104
Drum-rhythm similar to No. 18

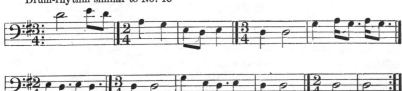

Analysis.—This melody progresses chiefly by whole tones, these constituting 73 per cent of the intervals. (See No. 28.)   G is regarded as the keynote, the song containing this tone with its second, fifth, and sixth.   The melody begins with an upward progression, though the general trend is downward.

PLOTS OF HAND GAME SONGS

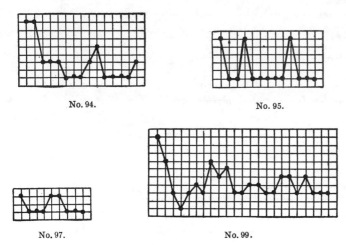

No. 94.

No. 95.

No. 97.

No. 99.

FIG. 17.—Plots, Group 13 (Hand game songs)

The plots of these songs show an emphasis on the lowest tone which is lacking in other groups and which recalls the plots of the songs of Sioux medicine men confident of their power.

HAND GAME SONGS

MELODIC ANALYSIS

TABLE 1F.—TONALITY

	Number of songs	Serial Nos. of songs
Major tonality	7	9', 95, 96, 97, 98, 99, 101.
Third lacking	2	100, 102.
Total	9	

TABLE 2F.—FIRST NOTE OF SONG—ITS RELATION TO KEYNOTE

	Number of songs	Serial Nos. of songs
Beginning on the—		
Octave	3	94, 99, 102.
Fifth	2	95, 101.
Third	3	96, 97, 98.
Keynote	1	100.
Total	9	

TABLE 3F.—LAST NOTE OF SONG—ITS RELATION TO KEYNOTE

	Number of songs	Serial Nos. of songs
Ending on the—		
Fifth	2	96, 100.
Third	1	97.
Keynote	6	94, 95, 98, 99, 101, 102.
Total	9	

TABLE 4F.—LAST NOTE OF SONG—ITS RELATION TO COMPASS OF SONG

	Number of songs	Serial Nos. of songs
Songs in which final tone is—		
Lowest tone in song	6	94, 96, 98, 100, 101, 102.
Immediately preceded by major third below	1	97.
Songs containing a minor third below the final tone	1	99.
Songs containing a semitone below the final tone	1	95.
Total	9	

HAND GAME SONGS—Continued

MELODIC ANALYSIS—continued

TABLE 5F.—NUMBER OF TONES COMPRISING COMPASS OF SONG

	Number of songs	Serial Nos. of songs
Compass of—		
Nine tones	2	99, 102.
Eight tones	1	94.
Six tones	3	95, 96, 100.
Five tones	2	95, 101.
Three tones	1	98.
Total	9	

TABLE 6F.—TONE MATERIAL

	Number of songs	Serial Nos. of songs
Fourth five-toned scale	1	99.
Major triad	2	97, 101.
Major triad and seventh	1	95.
Major triad and second	2	94, 96.
First, fourth, and fifth tones	1	100.
First, second, fifth, and sixth tones	1	102.
First, second, and third tones	1	98.
Total	9	

TABLE 7F.—ACCIDENTALS

	Number of songs	Serial Nos. of songs
Songs containing no accidentals	9	

TABLE 8F.—STRUCTURE

	Number of songs	Serial Nos. of songs
Melodic	4	98, 99, 100, 102.
Harmonic	5	94, 95, 96, 97, 101.
Total	9	

TABLE 9F.—FIRST PROGRESSION—DOWNWARD AND UPWARD

	Number of songs	Serial Nos. of songs
Downward	6	94, 95, 96, 98, 100, 101.
Upward	3	97, 99, 102.
Total	9	

HAND GAME SONGS—Continued

MELODIC ANALYSIS—continued

TABLE 10F.—TOTAL NUMBER OF PROGRESSIONS—DOWNWARD AND UPWARD

	Number of songs	Serial Nos. of songs
Downward	127	
Upward	96	
Total	223	

TABLE 11F.—INTERVALS IN DOWNWARD PROGRESSION

	Number of songs	Serial Nos. of songs
Interval of a—		
Fifth	1	
Fourth	20	
Major third	30	
Minor third	29	
Major second	45	
Minor second	2	
Total	127	

TABLE 12F.—INTERVALS IN UPWARD PROGRESSION

	Number of songs	Serial Nos. of songs
Interval of a—		
Fifth	5	
Fourth	17	
Major third	21	
Minor third	16	
Major second	35	
Minor second	2	
Total	96	

TABLE 13F.—AVERAGE NUMBER OF SEMITONES IN AN INTERVAL

Total number of intervals... 223
Total number of semitones... 730
Average number of semitones in an interval.. 3.2

HAND GAME SONGS—Continued

MELODIC ANALYSIS—continued

TABLE 14F.—KEY

	Number of songs	Serial Nos. of songs
Key of—		
A major	1	96.
D major	1	94.
E flat major	1	99.
E major	1	98.
G major	2	95, 97.
A flat major	1	101.
Third lacking	2	100, 102.
Total	9	

RHYTHMIC ANALYSIS

TABLE 15F.—PART OF MEASURE ON WHICH SONG BEGINS

	Number of songs	Serial Nos. of songs
Beginning on unaccented part of measure	2	96, 97.
Beginning on accented part of measure	7	94, 95, 98, 99, 100, 101, 102.
Total	9	

TABLE 16F.—RHYTHM (METER) OF FIRST MEASURE

	Number of songs	Serial Nos. of songs
First measure in—		
2–4 time	5	94, 95, 96, 98, 101.
3–4 time	4	97, 99, 100, 102.
Total	9	

TABLE 17F.—CHANGE OF TIME—MEASURE-LENGTHS

	Number of songs	Serial Nos. of songs
Songs containing no change of time	2	98, 100.
Songs containing a change of time	7	94, 95, 96, 97, 99, 101, 102.
Total	9	

Hand Game Songs—Continued

RHYTHMIC ANALYSIS—continued

Table 18f.—RHYTHM (METER) OF DRUM

	Number of songs	Serial Nos. of songs
Eighth notes unaccented	5	95, 96, 97, 98, 102.
Sixteenth notes unaccented	1	100.
Drum not recorded	3	94, 99, 101.
Total	9	

Table 19f.—RHYTHMIC UNIT OF SONG

	Number of songs	Serial Nos. of songs
Songs containing—		
No rhythmic unit	3	97, 99, 102.
One rhythmic unit	6	94, 95, 96, 98, 100, 101.
Total	9	

Table 20f.—TIME UNIT OF VOICE (AT BEGINNING OF SONG)

	Number of songs	Serial Nos. of songs
Metronome—		
60	1	99.
63	1	100.
76	1	101.
92	1	97.
96	1	94.
100	1	96.
104	1	102.
112	1	98.
120	1	95.
Total	9	

Table 21f.—TIME UNIT OF DRUM

	Number of songs	Serial Nos. of songs
Metronome—		
63	1	100.
100	1	96.
104	1	102.
112	1	98.
116	1	97.
120	1	95.
Drum not recorded	3	94, 99, 101.
Total	9	

Hand Game Songs—Continued

rhythmic analysis—continued

TABLE 22F.—COMPARISON OF TIME UNIT OF VOICE AND DRUM

	Number of songs	Serial Nos. of songs
Time unit of voice and drum the same............................	5	95, 96, 98, 100, 102.
Voice slower than drum..	1	97.
Drum not recorded..	3	94, 99, 101.
Total..	9	

MISCELLANEOUS SONGS

The three songs next following were called "smoking songs" and were recorded by Kolorow, a member of the Uncompahgre band of Utes. Kolorow stated that the first of the songs (No. 103) was sung by a party of men on their way to the lodge of the chief. On their arrival the chief lit a pipe and offered it to each man in turn. The men were seated in a circle on the ground and the second song (No. 104) was sung. After they had smoked for a while they stood in a circle and sang the third song of the group (No. 105).

No. 103. Smoking Song (a)   (Catalogue No. 781)

Recorded by SINGER No. 21

Voice ♩ = 120
Drum ♩ = 120
Drum-rhythm similar to No. 20

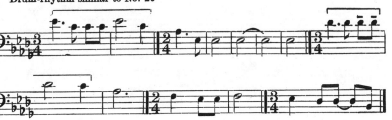

Analysis.—This song is irregular in its melodic structure, but is classified according to the latter portion, which contains the triad of B flat minor. All the tones of the octave except the sixth are present in the melody, which has a compass of 11 tones. About three-fourths of the intervals are minor thirds and major seconds.

No. 104. Smoking Song (b)   (Catalogue No. 782)

Recorded by SINGER No. 21

VOICE ♩ = 84
DRUM ♩ = 84
Drum-rhythm similar to No. 20

Analysis.—Harmonic in structure, this melody contains only the tones of the minor triad and fourth. It has a range of nine tones and contains 32 progressions, more than half of which are a major third or larger than a major third.

No. 105. Smoking Song (c)   (Catalogue No. 783)

Recorded by SINGER No. 21

VOICE ♩ = 72
DRUM ♩ = 72
Drum-rhythm similar to No. 100

Analysis.—This song opens with the same phrase which formed the rhythmic unit of the preceding song, but as there is no phrase resembling it in the remainder of the song it is not considered a rhythmic unit. The compass of the song is only six tones, this being much smaller than that of the preceding songs. The melody tones are those of the fourth five-toned scale. A rapid drumbeat characterizes the song, only one other song of this series (No. 100) having the same drum rhythm.

In explanation of the following song it was said that "when an Indian had a little tobacco which he had gotten from a white man the other Indians went to his house and sang this song. Then he would give them some of the tobacco. Afterwards they would go and sing somewhere else.''

No. 106. Song when begging for tobacco
(Catalogue No. 727)

Recorded by SINGER No. 16

VOICE ♩ = 72
DRUM ♩ = 72
Drum-rhythm similar to No. 18

Analysis.—Six renditions of this song were recorded, the last three being like the transcription and the others differing slightly in the fourth and fifth measures from the end. The song is melodic in structure, has a compass of 12 tones, and contains the major triad and second. The principal interval is the major second, comprising 71 per cent of the intervals. (See No. 24.) The song contains no rhythmic unit and is not rhythmic in general character.

The following song was sung on the arrival of visitors. The informant said: "We sang this song in the old days to show that we were glad to see our visitors. Then they gave us presents—a horse, a rifle, or a buffalo robe." [26]

No. 107. Song when welcoming visitors (Catalogue No. 728)

Recorded by SINGER No. 16

VOICE ♩ = 80
DRUM ♩ = 80
Drum-rhythm similar to No. 20

Analysis.—This song is characterized by the interval of the fourth, one-third of the intervals being fourths. The song has no rhythmic

---

[26] Before recording the song on the phonograph the singer recorded a few sentences which were translated. In these he said that after the singing of this song it was always customary to give a present, and as the writer was a visitor he hoped that the usual custom would be observed. The writer accordingly presented him with a small American flag.

interest, which may account for the fact that the renditions differ in tone values, the transcription being from the first rendition. In structure the song is melodic, in tonality it is major, and it contains all the tones of the octave except the sixth and seventh. It has a compass of seven tones.

The two songs next following were said to have been sung to an accompaniment of pounding on a rawhide. The rhythm of this pounding is different from that of the drumbeat in the other Ute songs under analysis. This rhythm is transcribed with song No. 108. The unaccented stroke of the drummer's stick is in the nature of a *rebound* and might be expected when the pounding is upon a stiff but unstretched material. A similar rhythm was noted among the Chippewa and described in Bulletin 45, page 6, as follows: "In beginning the rhythm of the woman's dance, the drummers give the unaccented beat with a rebound of the stick, so that it seems to be connected with the beat which precedes rather than that which follows it. As soon as the rhythm is well established, however, the unaccented beat clearly connects itself with the succeeding beat." Thus the rhythm of the drum at the opening of a certain performance was as described above, and changing to the rhythm noted with No. 36 of this series. This rhythm is further considered in Bulletin 53, page 10, the observation being made that the rhythm is similar to that of the adult heart. The rhythm occurs with only two Chippewa songs (Nos. 11 and 12, Bull. 53). These are the songs of a war messenger and the song which was sung on his return.

Concerning the preparation of the rawhide used with the Ute songs it was said that two large buffalo hides were sewed together and allowed to dry, so that they were very stiff. Holes were cut at intervals along the edge and a thong passed through the holes. Both men and women stood around the rawhide holding the thong with the left hand and pounding the rawhide with a stick held in the right hand. Often 10 or 12 persons stood around the rawhide.

When singing No. 108, a party of men carried the rawhide from tent to tent. No gifts were expected, the song being one of the "serenades" which are noted among numerous tribes.

No. 108. Serenade

(Catalogue No. 729)

Recorded by SINGER No. 16

Analysis.—This song is harmonic in structure and contains the tones of the fourth five-toned scale. It progresses chiefly by whole tones, about 61 per cent of the intervals being major seconds. (See No. 24.) The fourth is also a prominent interval.

The singer who recorded the following song did not describe it as a "serenade." He said that men and women stood around the rawhide, and that "they did this only once in a while in a large village, at night."

No. 109. Song around a rawhide   (Catalogue No. 785)

Recorded by SINGER No. 2

VOICE ♩ = 96
BEATING ON RAWHIDE ♩ = 96
Rhythm similar to No. 108

Analysis.—In this song the fourth is raised a semitone. The song contains all the tones of the octave except the seventh and is harmonic in structure. The progressions number 44, somewhat more than the usual number in Ute songs. Only four of these intervals are larger than a minor third.

The following is an example of an old dream song. As indicated in the songs of the Bear dance, it is not unusual for young men at the present time to "receive songs in dreams." (See p. 60.) This song, however, was recorded by Kanav (pl. 10, *b*), an aged man, who said that his uncle "dreamed" it and that he used to sing it when he was alone. The words were not recorded, but were said to mean "We are playing along the shore."

No. 110. Dream Song   (Catalogue No. 799)

Recorded by SINGER No. 23

Analysis.—Four renditions of this little melody were recorded without a break in the time. The keynote is A, and the melody contains only this tone and its second, third, and sixth—a tone material not occurring in the songs previously analyzed by the writer. More than 65 per cent of the progressions are whole tones. (See No. 28.) Part of the melody lies above and part below the keynote. Two rhythmic units occur, the first in triple and the second in double time.

PLOTS OF MISCELLANEOUS SONGS

This group of songs is diversified in character and the plots show no prevailing type. The following outlines are interesting in their variety and may be compared with the corresponding songs:

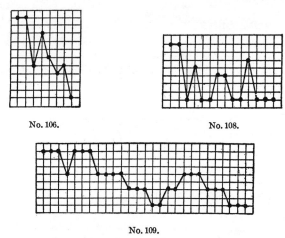

No. 106.   No. 108.

No. 109.

FIG. 18.—Plots, Group 14 (Miscellaneous songs).

Parade and Miscellaneous Songs

MELODIC ANALYSIS

TABLE 1G.—TONALITY

	Number of songs	Serial Nos. of songs
Major tonality	16	83, 84, 85, 86, 87, 88, 89, 90, 92, 93, 105, 106, 107, 108, 109, 110.
Minor tonality	3	91, 103, 104.
Total	19	

TABLE 2G.—FIRST NOTE OF SONG—ITS RELATION TO KEYNOTE

	Number of songs	Serial Nos. of songs
Beginning on the—		
Eleventh	1	103.
Ninth	2	85, 88.
Octave	4	92, 93, 106, 109.
Fifth	8	83, 84, 86, 87, 90, 104, 105, 108.
Third	3	89, 107, 110.
Keynote	1	91.
Total	19	

TABLE 3G.—LAST NOTE OF SONG—ITS RELATION TO KEYNOTE

	Number of songs	Serial Nos. of songs
Ending on the—		
Fifth	11	83, 84, 86, 87, 88, 89, 93, 104, 106, 107, 108.
Keynote	8	85, 90, 91, 92, 103, 105, 109, 110.
Total	19	

TABLE 4G.—LAST NOTE OF SONG—ITS RELATION TO COMPASS OF SONG

	Number of songs	Serial Nos. of songs
Songs in which final tone is—		
Lowest tone in song	16	83, 84, 85, 86, 87, 88, 89, 90, 91, 92, 93, 103, 105, 106, 108, 109.
Immediately preceded by whole tone below	1	104.
Songs containing a minor third below the final tone	1	110.
Songs containing a whole tone below the final tone	1	107
Total	19	

PARADE AND MISCELLANEOUS SONGS—Continued

MELODIC ANALYSIS—continued

TABLE 5G.—NUMBER OF TONES COMPRISING COMPASS OF SONG

	Number of songs	Serial Nos. of songs
Compass of—		
Twelve tones	3	87, 88, 106.
Eleven tones	2	93, 103.
Ten tones	2	85, 89.
Nine tones	2	83, 86.
Eight tones	7	84, 90, 91, 92, 104, 108, 109.
Seven tones	1	107.
Six tones	2	105, 110.
Total	19	

TABLE 6G.—TONE MATERIAL

	Number of songs	Serial Nos. of songs
Second five-toned scale	1	91.
Fourth five-toned scale	3	87, 105, 108.
Major triad and fourth	1	92.
Major triad and second	4	84, 88, 93, 106.
Minor triad and fourth	1	104.
Octave complete	1	89.
Octave complete except seventh	5	83, 85, 90, 103, 109.
Octave complete except seventh and sixth	1	107.
Octave complete except fourth	1	86.
First, second, third, and sixth tones	1	110.
Total	19	

TABLE 7G.—ACCIDENTALS

	Number of songs	Serial Nos. of songs
Songs containing—		
No accidentals	17	83, 84, 85, 86, 87, 88, 89, 90, 92, 93, 103, 104, 105, 106, 107, 108, 110.
Seventh raised a semitone	1	91.
Fourth raised a semitone	1	109.
Total	19	

PARADE AND MISCELLANEOUS SONGS—Continued

MELODIC ANALYSIS—continued

TABLE 8G.—STRUCTURE

	Number of songs	Serial Nos. of songs
Melodic	9	83, 86, 87, 90, 103, 105, 106, 107, 110.
Melodic with harmonic framework	6	84, 85, 88, 89, 91, 93.
Harmonic	4	92, 104, 108, 109.
Total	19	

TABLE 9G.—FIRST PROGRESSION—DOWNWARD AND UPWARD

	Number of songs	Serial Nos. of songs
Downward	14	83, 84, 85, 86, 87, 88, 89, 92, 93, 103, 104, 105, 107, 110.
Upward	5	90, 91, 106, 108, 109.
Total	19	

TABLE 10G.—TOTAL NUMBER OF PROGRESSIONS—DOWNWARD AND UPWARD

	Number of songs	Serial Nos. of songs
Downward	339	
Upward	214	
Total	553	

TABLE 11G.—INTERVALS IN DOWNWARD PROGRESSION

	Number of songs	Serial Nos. of songs
Interval of a—		
Fifth	4	
Fourth	64	
Major third	35	
Minor third	55	
Major second	170	
Minor second	11	
Total	339	

PARADE AND MISCELLANEOUS SONGS--Continued

MELODIC ANALYSIS—continued

TABLE 12G.—INTERVALS IN UPWARD PROGRESSION

	Number of songs	Serial Nos. of songs
Ninth	1	
Octave	1	
Seventh	1	
Major sixth	2	
Minor sixth	2	
Fifth	23	
Fourth	42	
Major third	22	
Minor third	21	
Major second	93	
Minor second	6	
Total	214	

TABLE 13G.—AVERAGE NUMBER OF SEMITONES IN AN INTERVAL

Number of intervals... 553
Number of semitones... 1,789
Average number of semitones in an interval................................... 3

TABLE 14G.—KEY

	Number of songs	Serial Nos. of songs
A major	1	110.
B flat major	1	109.
B flat minor	1	103.
C major	3	85, 87, 89
D major	2	88, 90.
E flat major	2	93, 106.
E major	2	83, 105.
F major	2	92, 107.
F sharp minor	1	91.
G major	1	86.
A flat major	2	84, 108.
G sharp minor	1	104.
Total	19	

TABLE 15G.—PART OF MEASURE ON WHICH SONG BEGINS

	Number of songs	Serial Nos. of songs
Beginning on unaccented part of measure	15	83, 84, 85, 87, 88, 89, 91, 92, 103, 104, 105, 106, 107, 108, 109.
Beginning on accented part of measure	4	86, 90, 93, 110.
Total	19	

PARADE AND MISCELLANEOUS SONGS—Continued

RHYTHMIC ANALYSIS

TABLE 16G.—RHYTHM (METER) OF FIRST MEASURE

	Number of songs	Serial Nos. of songs
First measure in—		
2–4 time	12	83, 85, 88, 89, 90, 91, 93, 105, 106, 107, 108, 109.
3–4 time	7	84, 86, 87, 92, 103, 104, 110.
Total	19	

TABLE 17G.—CHANGE OF TIME, MEASURE-LENGTHS

	Number of songs	Serial Nos. of songs
Songs containing no change in time	19	

TABLE 18G.—RHYTHM (METER) OF DRUM

	Number of songs	Serial Nos. of songs
Eighth notes unaccented	3	90, 105, 106.
Quarter notes unaccented	6	84, 89, 91, 103, 104, 107.
Each beat followed by an unaccented beat corresponding approximately to one count of a triplet	2	108, 109.
Rapid beat resembling a tremolo at opening of song, followed by a quarter-note beat	3	86, 87, 88.
Drum not recorded	5	83, 85, 92, 93, 105.
Total	19	

TABLE 19G.—RHYTHMIC UNIT OF SONG

	Number of songs	Serial Nos. of songs
Songs containing—		
No rhythmic unit	11	86, 89, 90, 91, 92, 93, 104, 105, 106, 107, 108.
One rhythmic unit	6	83, 84, 85, 88, 103, 109.
Two rhythmic units	1	110.
Three rhythmic units	1	87.
Total	19	

Parade and Miscellaneous Songs—Continued

RHYTHMIC ANALYSIS—continued

TABLE 20G.—TIME UNIT OF VOICE

	Number of songs	Serial Nos. of songs
Metronome—		
60	1	89.
63	2	83, 87.
66	4	84, 86, 88, 89.
72	3	105, 106, 108.
80	2	90, 107.
84	1	104.
92	1	85.
96	1	109.
120	2	108, 110.
132	2	91, 92.
Total	19	

TABLE 21G.—TIME UNIT OF DRUM [1]

	Number of songs	Serial Nos. of songs
Metronome—		
60	1	89.
63	1	87.
66	3	84, 86, 88.
72	1	108.
80	2	90, 107.
84	1	104.
96	1	109.
104	2	105, 106.
120	1	103.
132	1	91.
Drum not recorded	5	83, 85, 92, 93, 110.
Total	19	

TABLE 22G.—COMPARISON OF TIME UNIT OF VOICE AND DRUM

	Number of songs	Serial Nos. of songs
Time unit of voice and drum the same	13	84, 86, 87, 88, 89, 90, 91, 103, 104, 106, 107, 108, 109.
Voice slower than drum	1	105.
Drum not recorded	5	83, 85, 92, 93, 110.
Total	19	

[1] A tremolo drumbeat preceded the even drumbeat in Nos. 86, 87, 88. (See analysis of No. 72.)

RUDIMENTARY SONGS

The repetitions of the preceding songs show them to be entities, having a beginning and ending, and clearly remembered by the singer. The following material is different and may be called "the stuff of which songs are made." It has no definite ending and the performance could probably have been continued indefinitely. The transcription is closed at a convenient point in the melody. A rhythmic feeling is evident, but there is no repeated unit of rhythm except in the first song. The melodic formation is largely on a major triad. It appears as though the tones of a major triad were in the singer's consciousness and he made combinations of these and other tones as suited his fancy. The intonation on the octave, or *boundary* of the melody, was reasonably good, the fifth was somewhat less assured, and in many instances the other intervals can be indicated only approximately by musical notation. The several singers had no hesitation in beginning the songs, seeming as familiar with this variable form of musical expression as younger singers with the conventional song. The three old women who recorded these songs were in the room at the same time and each seemed to concur in the others' performance. There was no opportunity to learn whether they could duplicate these performances at a later time, but it seems extremely doubtful that they could have done so with any degree of exactness. It was said that the accompanying stories were narrated to the music. Thus, if the narrator changed the words of the story, he would probably vary the music accordingly.

All these stories are about animals, and we note in the music a suggestion of the characteristic of the animals, though this comparison can not safely be pressed too far. In song (a), which is said to have been sung by the prairie dogs, the tempo is rapid and the movement of the melody can be described as agile. Song (b) also is in rapid tempo and concerns a race between the tadpoles and the mice. In song (c) the motion of the story is less marked, but the tempo of the song is the same as in song (a). Only a portion of the cylinder is transcribed, as the phrases after the change of time were repeated over and over with slight changes that are not interesting. Song (d) presents a much slower tempo and a heavier type of melody. The accompanying story is that of the bear who stole the wolf's wife. In this, as in song (c), a large part of the phonographic cylinder contains only the phrases which appear in the latter part of the transcription and which are repeated in varied but unimportant forms.

Wiyu'tš (pl. 11, *b*), an aged woman who recorded the first three of these songs, said that she learned them from her mother up in the canyon. When she was a little girl her mother sang them to her and told her of the time when "the wolves were people." That was when her mother's grandfather was alive. She said that "the wolves worked at all the industries. Both the men and women worked, and when the woman got tired the man took his turn and worked. Each worked five times in a day when they were smart. The wolf-man made a rabbit trap and tanned the hides so they were soft for blankets and clothing. He had a stone knife. His wife wove cloth of bark. They ate chokecherries and lived in a house woven like a birds' nest. Their dishes were made of sand and dirt. They made kettles of sand and dirt and boiled meat in them. They also made frying pans and plates. After they made these things they had a fire, and when the fire was red they put the dishes in the fire for a long time, which made them hard and strong. Their bread was baked in the ashes, and they had nice white bread. Sometimes they made bread out of chokecherries."

In addition to the songs which are transcribed Wiyu'tš recorded a song which she said the wolves sang, but by an unfortunate accident the cylinder was broken before the song could be transcribed.

STORY OF THE PRAIRIE DOGS

The following story was sung to the melody transcribed as "Rudimentary Song (a)."

Once the prairie dogs and the wildcats were all white. There was a prairie-dog man who wanted a wildcat woman to run away with him. At first she did not like him, but afterwards she ran away with him. Her mother did not want her to marry the prairie dog because he did not hunt. Her mother wanted her to marry the magpie, who hunted and got rabbits and other animals. So the mother went and took her daughter away from the prairie dog and gave her to the magpie, who gave his mother-in-law everything that he got in the hunt. They lived up in the mountain. The mother-in-law told the prairie dog that he was of no use because he lived in the ground.

Rudimentary Song (a)

STORY OF THE FROG'S CHILDREN

This story was related in song, a portion of the melody being transcribed. The story, in the words of the interpreter, is as follows:

The frog ate a great deal, and so he was very fat. The jack rabbit was as big as a dog, and he bit the frog on the face and leg. The frog was so fat he could not run away. The rabbit shook the frog and said, "You can't make me let go." Then the frog said, "Yes, I can."

Afterwards the frog's little children (tadpoles) ran races with a mouse. Before the race they shook hands, and the mouse said, "You can't beat me, you have such fat tails"; but the frog's little children won the race.

Rudimentary Song (b)

STORY OF THE RED BUG AND THE FOX

The story narrated to this melody was as follows: A red bug on the ground stung a fox so that he could not lie down. When he awoke he cried with pain all the time. He cried every hour. The fox was not afraid of the bug. He stayed close to the bug all the time and said to the bug, "Good morning; wake up," quite early in the morning. Then the bug wanted the fox to dance with her. The

fox said, "No, we can't do that; go to sleep." She said, "I can't."
He said, "Yes you will, yes you will." He said it twice. She said,
,'Good morning, sir; good morning, sir."

Rudimentary Song (c)

The following story was related and its song recorded by Fanny
Provo (singer No. 13).

STORY OF THE BEAR WHO STOLE THE WOLF'S WIFE

A bear came and stole the wolf's wife. She had a little baby.
The baby cried, and so the father wolf followed the bear's tracks
and found the mother wolf. The bear was very angry and began
to fight with the wolf, but the wolf threw him on the ground and
took the mother wolf away. The bear had told the wolf that her
husband could not beat him, but the wolf threw the bear on the
ground and beat him. The little wolf baby cried and screamed while
his father was away. He was glad to see his mother and ran to her.
The mother wolf did not want to leave the bear, but her husband
made her come back with him.

Rudimentary Song (d)

PLOTS OF RUDIMENTARY SONGS

A different method has been used in the "plotting" of the rudimentary songs. Heavy horizontal lines are used to represent the
keynote and its octave, a light dotted line represents the third, and a
heavy broken line represents the fifth. On these horizontal lines the

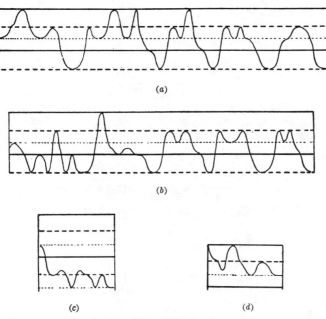

(a)

(b)

(c)   (d)

FIG. 19.—Plots, Group 15 (Rudimentary songs)

progression of the accented melody tones is plotted by means of a
curved line. It will be noted that, with few exceptions, the accented
tones occur on the intervals represented by horizontal lines. Accented tones occurring on other intervals are represented by curves
at approximately the correct distance between the horizontal lines.

APPENDIX

In order to test the accuracy of certain observations concerning the relative rhythms of voice and drum in Indian songs, the writer secured the courteous cooperation of Dr. Dayton C. Miller, head of the department of physics, Case School of Applied Science, Cleveland, Ohio. The phonograph on which the Ute songs were recorded was taken to Cleveland, together with phonographic records made on the reservation. These records had already been transcribed by ear, the only instruments of measurement being the piano for the pitch of the tones and a standardized metronome for their time duration. The phonograph was installed in Dr. Miller's laboratory (pl. 12), portions of two records were played by the phonograph, and the

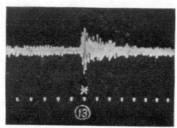

FIG. 20.—Photograph of drumbeat

sound recorded graphically by the phonodeik. (See pl. 13.) The accompanying analyses of the photographs, kindly prepared by Dr. Miller, show the result of the test. A full consideration of the phonodeik, invented by Dr. Miller, is contained in "The Science of Musical Sounds." [27]

ANALYTICAL STUDY OF PHOTOGRAPHS TAKEN WITH THE PHONODEIK

WOMAN'S DANCE—NO. 37

A portion of the music of the Woman's dance, of about 23 seconds' duration, as reproduced by the phonograph, was photographed with the phonodeik, making a film record about 38 feet long. The part of the song which is photographed begins when the stylus of the reproducer of the phonograph is about $2\frac{9}{16}$ inches from the beginning end of the wax cylinder record; it is at the beginning of a new stanza of the song. [A portion of this photograph, with its musical transcription, is shown in pl. 14.]

---

[27] Miller, Dayton Clarence, The Science of Musical Sounds. New York, 1916, pp. 78–88.

LABORATORY OF DR. DAYTON C. MILLER, SHOWING PHONOGRAPH AND PHONODEIK

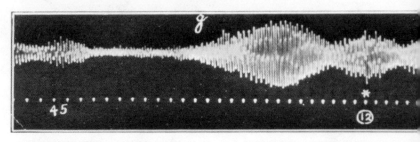

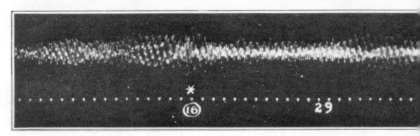

a, Tone photographs of portions of Woman

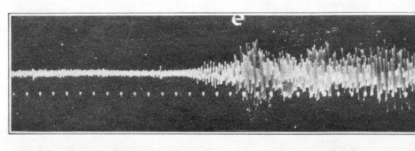

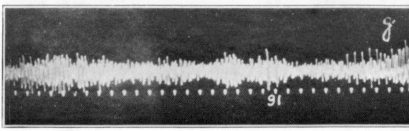

b, Tone photographs of close of second and all of third

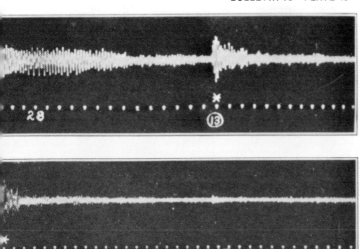

Drumbeats at 13 and 17.

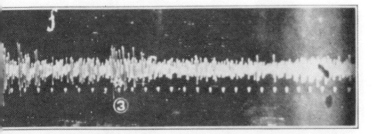

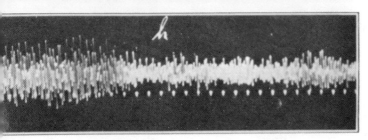

ne dance song.   (Sections *e* to *h*, pl. 16)

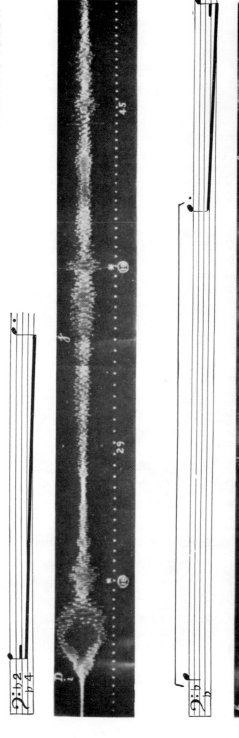

Transcription of portions of Woman's dance song (sections *i* to *l*), with tone photograph of corresponding portion

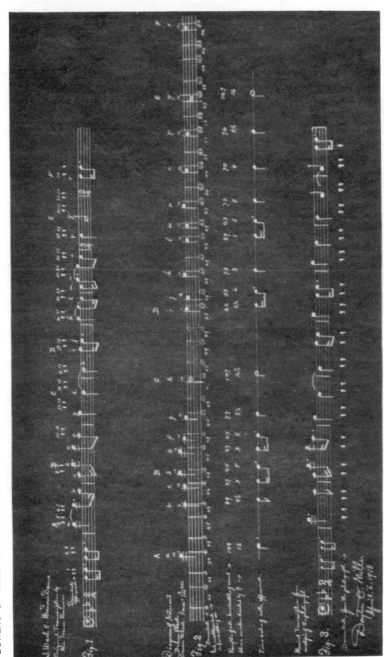

Transcriptions of portion of Woman's dance song (No. 37, measures 1 to 9), with diagram

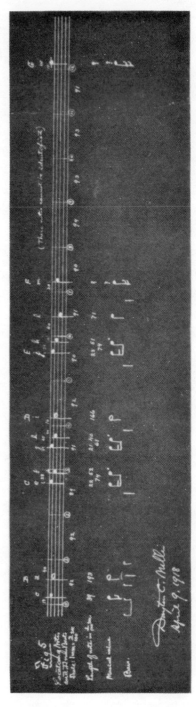

Transcriptions of portion of Lame dance song (duplication of No. 37, measures 8 to 15), with diagram

The first purpose of the study was to determine the relation of the drumbeats to the accents of the voice. In the photograph there are 62 drumbeats, which are indicated on the photograph by white *'s, and they are numbered consecutively by numerals in circles as ③. The effect of the drumbeat is to produce a short series of vibrations of the general pattern shown in figure 20.

When the voice is very soft or silent, the drum record is as shown at ⑬ and ⑰; when it is superposed on the voice, the effect is shown by a few extra wide vibrations, as at ①, ③, and ⑤. By careful study it has been possible to identify all of the drumbeats, though some of them are faint.

The dots in a row below the sound record are time signals one one-hundredth second apart. In taking this photograph the film was moved by hand, resulting in a varying speed; when the dots are nearer together, the corresponding speed is slower. The numerals between the *'s are the time intervals between the drumbeats in hundredths of a second.

The first study of the photograph shows a remarkable regularity in the rhythmic beats of the drum. The beats occur in pairs following an accented tone of the voice; 30 pairs are shown on the photo-

Ratio of 2:3   ● ●   ● ●   ● ●   ● ●   ●

Ratio of 1:2   ● ●   ● ●   ● ●   ● ●

FIG. 21.—Ratios of drumbeats

graph. The interval between the two beats of a pair is, in 17 instances, 0.29 second; there are six intervals of 0.28 second, four of 0.30 second, two of 0.27 second, and one of ‾0.31 second. The interval may then be said to be 0.29 second, with a variation rarely exceeding 0.01 second either way. The average of intervals between the pairs of beats is 0.45 second, there being seven of this length; there are 10 intervals of 0.44 second, five of 0.46 second, three of 0.43 second, and five of 0.47 second. Thus the average interval between pairs is 0.45 second, the variation from this value rarely being more than 0.01 second and never being more than 0.02 second. The ratio of the interval between the two beats of a pair to the interval between pairs is almost exactly 2:3, and this ratio is maintained with mechanical regularity throughout the song. It was suggested that the drumbeats might be thought of as occurring in triplicate with one beat of each triplet omitted. This would require a ratio of 1:2. The difference between the two ratios is shown in the spacing of the dots in the following rows (fig. 21):

A further noticeable peculiarity is that the first beat of a pair of drumbeats follows the beginning of an accented voice tone with great regularity. Of 25 such instances identified on the photograph the drumbeat follows the voice by 0.12 second in 12 cases, and in no instance does the interval differ from this by more than 0.02 second.

A comparison has been made of a portion of the photographic record, about 20 feet long, between drumbeats ① and ㉞, with the phonograph reproduction timed with a stop watch. In this manner it was possible to locate the principal notes in exact time.

Figure 1 [pl. 15] is the music as originally submitted, transcribed from the phonographic record. The letters A, B, C, etc., indicate certain distinct notes of the phonographic rendition; the corresponding portions are marked with the same letters on the upper edge of the photograph. While listening to the phonograph the relation of the pairs of drumbeats to the music was noted by ear and roughly marked on the score thus: □'□'□'□'□'□'. Thirty-four of these beats are numbered on the score, and the same beats were identified on the photograph and correspondingly numbered. By noting the relation of the drumbeats to the notes of the score and by observing the variations in the width (loudness or rhythm) of the photographic record as related to the corresponding drumbeats on the photograph it is possible to locate the beginning of each note of the music. The corresponding notes of the score and the photograph are lettered $a, b, c-p, q, r$.

Figure 2 [pl. 15] is a diagram showing the exact time relations of the drumbeats and notes, as determined by counting the hundredths of seconds on the photograph. The spacing along the staff shows the exact time value of each note and the relation of each note to the drumbeats. The bars [marked ①, ②, ③, etc.] are the drumbeats, numbered as on the photograph, thus (8). The numbers between the circles are the intervals, in hundredths of a second, between the drumbeats. The numbers above the notes are the intervals, in hundredths of a second, between the beginning of the notes and the succeeding drumbeats, as counted on the photograph.

The numbers below the staff, as 109, 39, 27, etc., are the intervals between notes (length of notes) in hundredths of a second. Inspection shows that 9 is approximately a common divisor of this number, and for purposes of comparison they were divided by 9, the approximate results being given in the next row of figures, as 12, 4⅓, etc. These numbers are proportional to the lengths of the notes. Assuming 8 to correspond to a quarter note, the first note is a dotted quarter, and the second is an eighth note, etc. The interpretation of the lengths of the note in musical notation may then be written as in the last line of figure 2 [pl. 15], and inspection of this series enables the division of the notes into appropriate groups for the bars of music. This latter operation should properly be done in connection with the phrasing and rhythm of the words.

The pitches of the notes having been obtained from the transcribed record,[28] the completed musical transcription is obtained as given in figure 3 [pl. 15]. The revised location of the drumbeats is shown by the dots below the score.

One of the interesting results of the quantitative transcription of this phrase is the fact that it agrees so well with the original musical transcription. There is no essential difference. Perhaps the omission of the measure in 3-4 time is not justified, though the exact time value is as given in figure 3 [pl. 15]. A more extended study would certainly make possible an exact transcription of the whole song, but the close agreement of the two methods hardly justifies the great amount of labor involved in the photographic method. This study was undertaken principally to learn what could be done if it were desirable.

LAME DANCE—NO. 39

The portion of the music of the Lame dance of about 15 seconds' duration as reproduced by the phonograph was photographed with the phonodeik, making a film record about 19 feet long. The part of the song which is photographed begins when the stylus of the reproducer of the phonograph is about $2\frac{3}{16}$ inches from the beginning end of the wax cylinder record. The original musical transcription of the portion photographed is given in figure 4 [pl. 16]. The purpose of the study was to determine the relation of the drumbeats to the rhythm of the voice. The record of a drumbeat appears on the photograph as a short series of vibrations of the pattern shown in figure 20.

Thirteen consecutive drumbeats have been identified, and they have been marked by *'s and numbered by serial numbers in circles, as ①, ⑫.

The dots in a row below the sound record are time signals, one one-hundredth second apart. The numbers below the dots between the *'s are the time intervals between the drumbeats in hundredths of a second.

The notes of the music which have distinct accents as heard on the phonograph are marked A–G on both the score, figure 4 [pl. 16], and on the upper edge of the photograph. Each note of the score is marked with a letter, as a, b, c–w, and the same notes when identified are similarly marked on the photograph.

There is a remarkable regularity in the beats of the drum. The 12 intervals between beats, in hundredths of a second, are 92, 92,

---

[28] A certified test of the author's pitch discrimination was made in 1914 by Prof. Carl E. Seashore, dean of the Graduate College, University of Iowa, Iowa City, Iowa.

89, 91, 92, 90, 91, 90, 94, 93, 93, 91.   The average interval is 0.92 second.

Figure 5 [pl. 16] is a diagram of the time relations of the various elements of the music drawn to exact scale, 1 millimeter being equal to $\frac{3}{1000}$ second. The drumbeats are marked by bars and these and the notes are marked as already described. The numbers above the notes are the intervals in hundredths of a second between the beginning of the note and the preceding or succeeding drumbeat, as counted on the photograph. The numbers, as 39, 193, etc., are the intervals between notes (lengths of notes) in hundredths of a second. The note c is 0.39 second long; e and f together are 0.74 second long; g and h, 0.74 second long; and l, 0.71 second long. It would appear that a quarter note may be taken as equal to 0.74 second, exactly the same value as is very definitely shown to exist in the Woman's dance. The first note of the diagram is then an eighth note, the second is a dotted half note, etc. The interpretation of the length of the notes in musical notation may then be written as in the last line of figure 5 [pl. 16]. The phrase thus interpreted is hardly long enough to determine the length of the bar, but the piece seems to be in 2–4 time, with bars as indicated. This is in substantial agreement with the original tránscription.

From this study of the photograph of the Lame dance it is difficult to determine any definite relation between the drumbeats, which occur with mechanical regularity, and the voice, which has a varying accent and rhythm. Perhaps it may be said that a drumbeat follows an accented vocal note, as beats ③, ④, and ⑥ follow the accented notes ef, gh, and jk. On the other hand, the strongly accented note w follows beat ⑫ after a short interval of 0.11 second.

In the Woman's dance each pair of drumbeats seems to correspond very directly to the 2–4 measure of the musical notation, and such a measure has a length of $0.29 + 0.45 = 0.74$ second, which is the period of the pairs of beats. In the Lame dance the quarter note of the voice seems to be exactly the same as for the Woman's dance, 0.74 second, but in the Lame dance there is no apparent relation of this interval to the drumbeats, which are 0.92 second apart.

DAYTON C. MILLER.

APRIL 9, 1918.

INDEX

211